FOLK MUSIC
INSTRUMENTS

FOLK

MUSIC INSTRUMENTS

Alexander Buchner

CROWN

Title page: Musical bow. Cave painting
from the Stone Age, c. 15 000 BC, Trois
Frères, France

© 1972 Artia, Prague
First published in the United States of America 1972
by Crown Publishers, Inc.,
419 Park Avenue South, New York, New York 10016
Library of Congress Catalog Card Number 76–173297
Text by Alexander Buchner
Translated by Alžběta Nováková
Printed in Czechoslovakia by Svoboda

CONTENTS

INTRODUCTION

We have come a long way from the hunting bow which paleolithic man held between his teeth and plucked, turning it into a 'musical instrument'. Today, at the end of a long line of development there is the harp. The origins of all our present musical instruments were indeed most primitive. The picture of a man with an animal mask found on the walls of the Trois Frères cave in France shows that instrumental music was performed in prehistoric times. The earliest inhabitants of South Africa, the Bushmen of the Kalahari Desert, to this day use their hunting bow as a musical bow. It follows from this important finding that musical instruments have evolved from objects of daily use. The first stimulus was given by the use of sound when hunting, by the bow, by signalling whistles, by decoys, or in the performance of tribal rites, when, for example, the sound of the drum represented the voice of the deceased, and the bull-roarer that of the demons. For the magic of tone to affect the demons, sound itself is often sufficient in man's simple cultures. In exceptional cases this phenomenon also appears in more advanced cultures, as in the Chinese theatre, where important scenes are introduced by the irregular beating of gongs and bells, or in Tibet, where the same note is sounded for several minutes on end on long trumpets called dung chen (tung che).

Musical instruments were born at the moment when the reverberating object no longer had a purely tonal or magic function, and when man began to try and use it beyond its original function of imitating a certain sound. This occurred as early as prehistoric times, and it was then that man also realized that he could determine the pitch of the tone at will. He found that the shorter the sticks, whistle tubes, or strings, the higher the note they produced. Thus sticks of various length were joined into xylophones, tubes into panpipes and strings into zithers. The production of various notes on one whistle by boring fingerholes into it, or on strings by the player touching them at different points, marked the next step in development.

Quite apart from their musical purpose, right from the beginning musical instruments also had a decorative function, sometimes far more important to primitive man than the sounds they could produce. There existed many different ways of adorning a musical instrument. The simplest was to tie the ornament to it. But the purpose of this ornament was often not merely decorative. It also cast a certain reflection on the owner when, for example, trophies such as the bones of an animal killed in the chase or some other object gained in battle were used. Instruments were also adorned with wickerwork, bird's feathers or paintings. A very complicated development finally led to musical instruments serving not only the pleasure of hearing sound, but a mainly musical purpose.

Folk instruments, which in number, sound and variety of shape, far exceed instruments of European art music, are usually made by the country people themselves. This is in contrast to art music instruments, which are the work of specialized instrument makers or factories. The basis of solo parts played on folk instruments is formed by song and dance. Whereas in the performance of art music the audience plays a purely passive part, folk music in its true surroundings forms an inseparable entity with dancing. For the folk musician his performance on a musical instrument is the artistic reflection of his own life, an organic component of his environment, a specific occasion without which musical expression could not exist at all in his consciousness. It is not disciplined, sentimental music, full of pathos created for the audience, but music that arises at the very moment when the musician feels the inner need of expressing himself in this way. It is an intimate expression not looking for effect, nor subordinated to the taste of others. The folk style of reproduction on the whole is not pleasing to people used to the anachronic, romantic form of reproduction, it is far closer to an almost modern objective way of expression. And thus instrumental folk music must not be regarded as an archaic remnant of the past, but in its breadth, vitality and value as creating the rich instrumental culture of the nations, presenting the artistic reflection of their spiritual and sensual life which must be further developed and enriched.

Note must be taken, however, not only of folk instruments, but also of national instruments, i. e. instruments used by members of the nations of the world within their geographical or ethnical frontiers, though it is well known that at the present level of development and distribution of various types of instruments, no exact frontiers can be determined. Cultural development has never respected political, ethnical or other frontiers. Since time immemorial there has been a constant exchange of influence on cultural heritage and traditions, willingly or unwillingly, through trade contacts, wars, or the migration of nations. For example, in the course of history the Islamic peoples, from Morocco to Indonesia, have interchanged their musical instruments so frequently that today it is very difficult to say for certain where any one instrument was used first.

The manifold variety and abundance of types of existing musical instruments has always forced scientists and specialists to attempt a survey of all this wealth. So far none have succeeded in elaborating a classification which would fully solve the problem of a scheme of musical instruments. The classical musician prefers the categorization which for centuries has divided instruments into percussion, wind and string instruments. The technologist tries to classify instruments according to acoustic conditions, without regard to the historical development. The historian is in favour of the genetic viewpoint expressing the historical process of the formation of a musical instrument from its archetype to a certain group of instruments. From the position of regional ethnographical research it is most suitable to group the instruments according to the degree of skill necessary in their production. Not even E. M. Hornbostel's and C. Sachs's joint efforts to arrive at a scientific chronology of musical instruments which is generally accepted is without weak points. It therefore seems that a scheme of musical instruments will be most clearly arranged if drawn up according to acoustic principles, just as a survey of the musical instruments of the world will best permit a suitable link-up of geographical and historical views. The progression and spread of musical instruments points to the existence of certain production centres, above all in Asia, for it was here that new impulses constantly arose and from there that instruments spread to the most distant lands.

Musical instruments developed from those producing discordant sounds to those producing melodies, first in cultures of average development and then in the more mature cultures. They developed quickly in every direction. Society, developing at the dawn of the historical epoch of mankind towards the division of labour and stratification into classes,

'There was a dudka or sopilka, or svistilka. The young man played as well as he knew, and some Cossacks, and the other who had sat down in a circle, watched the piper as if they had never seen him before, listening with their whole bodies as if they had never heard anything like this before, as if he were a wonder for them. But he wasn't, for every one of them knew how to play just as well. This came out during the interval when everybody begged the boy to lend them his whistle. Everyone wanted to have a go himself. And the whistleflute went from hand to hand, or rather from mouth to mouth. And every time somebody started to play all the others again watched the piper like an apparition and listened to his playing with all their might.'

Ludvík Kuba, the Czech ethnographer, in his study 'Travelling through Eastern Europe'.

left the performance of music to special castes. In advanced cultures outside Europe instrumental music gained much ground, especially at the court, without excluding ritual music to such an extent, however, as happened in Europe. It is in modern society that the musical instrument has reached the zenith of its mission: to give expression to music for the joy of man.

SYSTEM OF MUSICAL INSTRUMENTS

MUSICAL INSTRUMENTS

ACOUSTIC ELECTRO-ACOUSTIC ELECTRIC AUTOMATOPHONIC
(with electric adapter)

IDIOPHONES	AEROPHONES	SYNPHONES
source of sound: firm elastic material	source of sound: air contained within walls of instrument	source of sound: material that becomes elastic by artificial stretching

IDIOPHONES

STICKS				SLABS
ying	suspended	fixed	lying	suspended
xylophones metallophones marimba tubaphone celesta, etc.	triangle bells, etc.	sansa Jew's harp sheng harmonika, etc.	castanets slit drums, etc.	lithophones cymbals gongs tam-tam, etc.

AEROPHONES

EDGE		MOUTHPIECE		REED	
without slit	with slit	conical bore	cylindrical bore	single reed	double reed
pan-pipe cross flute endblown flute, etc.	beaked flute Hawaiian flute fujara, etc.	horns bugles, etc.	trumpets trombones etc.	clarinets, etc.	oboe shawm, etc.

SYNPHONES

MEMBRANE		STRING	
tuned	without fixed pitch	with fixed tone series	with optional tone series
tympana some non-European drums	drums tambourines, etc.	harps dulcimers piano Aeolan harp, etc.	violins guitars lutes, etc.

EAST ASIA

CHINA

One of the main features of advanced cultures, for example China, is the formation of tonal systems dealing with the duration, pitch and intervals of tones. These are closely connected with musical instruments though in every cultural region usually only one instrument was used to establish the system. In China this was the zither *kin, tsisiantsin, qixianqin*, in India the chordophone *vina* and in the Islamic world the lute *'ud*. Vocal music did not contribute towards the formation of fixed norms since the human voice was not suitable to mark permanent tone relations. The importance of the tone systems to the full understanding of the music of the separate cultures and for the construction of musical instruments is therefore evident.

A feature common to all these tone systems is the view that numbers have a certain relation to the cosmos. The basis of this numerical mysticism is the belief in the existence of two proto-forces corresponding to the principle male — female, earthly — heavenly, light — dark, etc. Particular importance was attached to three numbers: one as a neutral number, two and three as the initial numbers of the series of odd and even. Since music was regarded as the expression of world harmony tonal relations had to be connected with the cosmological numbers. The first musicologist to discover that the intervals on musical instruments could be expressed by the numbers one, two and three must have felt a strange elation. When shortening a string or whistle tube by one third a tone is obtained which — together with the basic tone — gives one of the most frequently used combinations: the fifth. That the fifth on the string forms a somewhat larger interval than the fifth on a whistle tube could but did not throw any doubts on the validity of the laws whose reflection was music as the representative of world harmony. A means for the accurate determination of tonal relations was found by European science as late as in the nineteenth century in the form of frequencies. That the Chinese theoreticians had been able to deduce generally valid acoustic laws with the help of experiments on string instruments without a knowledge of frequencies was only possible because the metric norms were applied to musical instruments, the same metric norms that controlled the dimensions of the largest structures of ancient times.

Cosmological numbers and measures are the basis of the Chinese tonal system. Its most ancient form was probably the pentatonic scale without half-tones known to the Babylonians and the ancient Egyptians. Later on two supplementary were added to the five major tones used in practice in the modern Chinese notation for the zither *kin, tsisiantsin*. Legend has it that in the third millenium BC, Emperor Chuang-Ti ordered Ling-Lu, the scholar, to elaborate a firm theoretical basis for music. According to certain numerical relations, Ling-Lu made twelve bamboo whistles of varying length, corresponding in tone to the song of two magic birds living in the Emperor's garden. Arranged according to length these whistles represented the chromatic scale. Ling-Lu divided the pitch-pipes called lü (lü = origin, law, measure) according to the principle of male — female into a perfect or 'male' series (f to d sharp) and an imperfect or 'female' series (f sharp to d). This system, which was later to become the basis of Chinese musical theory, was perfected and more closely defined by many generations of scholars and music theoreticians. Hieroglyphics depicting strings and bamboo stems joined together have, since

TONAL SYSTEM

11

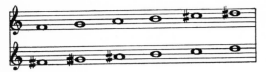

Tone series of the Chinese tonal series *lü*

IDIOPHONES

	d'''	
c#'''	b''	a''
e''	f#''	g''
d''	b'	a'

	d'''	
c#'''	b''	a''
g''	f#''	e''
d''	b'	a'

Distribution of gongs on the Chinese instrument *yün lo*

ancient times, represented the word *sychzhu* — music. Bamboo was contained in the symbol because it is an important raw material in the production of musical instruments. Music, according to the Chinese Canon of Documents, is 'song accompanied by instrumental music and dance movements'. The conception of music as the synthesis of tone, word and movement permeates the whole of Chinese philosophy and has stimulated the unusually strong development of musical instruments. Matter, in Chinese music, is far more than a means of producing a sound. Like body and soul, a material and its sound were manifestations of the same phenomenon. The longer the tone lasted, the better it was isolated, the more profoundly it was possible for the listener to penetrate into the substance that had produced it. This view caused great importance to be attached to idiophones that developed into instruments capable of melody (in European civilizations idiophones have played a subsidiary role).

The importance of idiophones among ancient Chinese instruments was confirmed by finds of lithophones in the course of archeological excavations. Though their age exceeds many thousands of years, they are of a high level of development. They include *shiking (siqing* i.e. stone king, *shi* = stone*)* of irregular rounded shape, and a number of tuned and suspended lithophones called *pien ch'ing (pienqing, bianking)*. Among the musical instruments forming part of the collection housed today in the Heavenly Temple at Peking, a *pien ch'ing* from the eighteenth century is to be found with sixteen tuned slabs of green nephrite. Today lithophones are used only in monasteries, for Confucius declared that 'a concert is complete when the large bell proclaims the commencement of the music, and the sonorous stone proclaims its close'. Enormous marble slabs, struck with heavy wooden clubs, are still to be found in Annamese temples.

Among ancient Chinese instruments must also be listed metallophones, a great variety of bells, gongs and cymbals, the sound of which enriched the performance of court orchestras. The cymbals *nao* form the transition to bells. They are shaped like elliptic cups with handles, and in ancient China were used as signalling instruments. The elliptical shape is still preserved by the bell *chung (jong, zhong)* struck from the outside with a disconnected hammer, and had a cylindrical protuberance instead of the usual crown, linked to the side with a handle from which the instrument was suspended. Another bell, *boh (bo)*, is round and has a hook instead of the crown so that it already hangs in a perpendicular position, in contrast to the *chung* which hangs in a slanting position. Several *chungs* differently tuned make up a bell chime, *pien, chung*. A tomb from the period of the Tsiango dynasty (403 — 221 BC) contained — among other musical instruments — also a bell chime consisting of thirteen *chungs* tuned to b, c sharp¹, d sharp¹, f sharp ¹, g sharp¹, a sharp¹, b¹, c sharp², d sharp², f sharp², g sharp², a², d sharp³, i.e. a B major scale with the fourth missing.

Bells of varying shapes and sizes played an important part in the lives of the Chinese people. Small bells were hung around the necks of domestic animals to protect them against evil spirits. Bells were suspended at doors, not to warn the owner of thieves, but to protect him against demons. Larger bells were supposed to attract rain and guarantee a good harvest. The largest bell in Peking was rung by the Emperor himself when he was praying for rain. The gong chime *yün lo (lo* = gong*)* made up usually of *sjaolo (hsialo)*, i.e. small gongs, was of Mongolian origin. The gongs were suspended in rows of three from a wooden frame; only the tenth gong was suspended independently at the highest point of the frame.

A xylophone of special construction is the trough, *chu*. The hammer, linked to a pivot inside on the bottom, is reached through a large hole on one side and strikes the bottom. It is used at the beginning of the Confucian service. This method of striking indicates that the instrument originated from a grain mortar. This explains why the bottom and not the outside wall is struck, which would be simpler and more natural. The *bangtzy* is a kind of clapper, probably from India. It consists of a block of hard wood played by striking with a cylindrical stick. There is another clapper, *pai pan*, used in orchestras of folk instruments to mark the accented beat. It is made of three or more wedge-shaped pieces of wood connected by a cord threaded through two small holes in each of the pieces. When playing, the musician holds the clapper by the upper edge of the pieces with the fingers of one hand and sets them in motion with a light flick of the wrist. A similar sound is produced by the scraper *yü*, the tiger, carved out of a piece of wood to represent a crouching tiger on a plinth. On the back of the animal is a dentated strip representing the spine. This is scraped with a split wand of bamboo. *Mu yü*, the wooden fish, a kind of bell without clapper, is carved out of camphor wood *(Camphora officinalis)*, fitted with a handle and decorated with carvings of strange shapes recalling the fins of a fish. This also gave the instrument its name. As a fish has no eyelids, it is the symbol of wakeful attention. When played the instrument is held by the handle, or placed on a soft cushion and struck with a heavy stick. When beaten, the wooden fish was supposed to attract the notice of the divinity. And since a fish lives in the water it was considered particularly efficacious with prayers for rain.

Archeological finds include a number of drums. Written records of the drum *ku* date back to the Jing (Yin) period (1401—1122 BC). In the Book of Songs Confucius describes the performance of a hymn to the accompaniment of drums. Wall paintings at Duenhwang record a number of different drums of which the drum *po fu*, that used to be filled with rice hulls, is still widely used today. The player suspends it from his neck and beats it with both hands. The temple musician holds it horizontally on the knees and at the end of each verse of the Confucian hymn beats it three times, once with the right hand on the right membrane *po*, then with the left hand on the left membrane *fu*, and for the third time with both hands on both membranes. In both folk and professional orchestras the drum *tang ku* is used. It is barrel-shaped, with a shallow wooden corpus. The heads are nailed to it on both sides. The drum *aogu*, with a deeper corpus, is similar to the *tang ku*. Two rings enable the player to suspend the *jaogu* from his shoulders. In the theatres of northern China the drum *shu ku (shugu)* is used which, as a folk instrument, is called *hsiao ku (sjaogu)*, i.e. small drum. It is placed on a high stand with three feet. With a shallow corpus but of very massive shape is the drum *tanggu (dangu)*, which appears in folk and theatre ensembles. It is interesting to note that the membrane is nailed not from the side, but from above. It is also called *khuajgu*, i.e. drum and is played with a longer stick. During all musical performances, whether solo or orchestral, the drum *bangu* (also *dangpig*), with a strong wooden body in the shape of an upturned goblet, is used. It has a small opening for sound at the bottom, is placed on a three-legged stand and played with two sticks by the leader of the ensemble.

Among the considerable number of chordophones the oldest are two zithers, to be found in varying shapes among all the peoples of Eastern and South Eastern Asia. These are the *shê* and the *kin (tsisiantsin, qixianqin, yangqin)*, both with a long, flat body and a large number of strings. According to legend the *shê* was invented by the Emperor Fu si and originally had fifty strings. Today only the zither *dashê* (i.e. big *shê*) with twenty-five strings or *hsiao shê* (i.e. small *shê*) with sixteen strings, is used. Two movable bridges reaching across the entire width of the board determine the length of the strings, which are fitted to the tail pins at the bottom of the body and tuned in various ways. The most frequent is d, e, f sharp, a, b, d^1, e^1, f sharp^1, a^1, b^1, d^2, e^2, f sharp^2, a^2, b^2, d^3. The *shê* is played with both hands, the left on the first twelve strings, the right on the others, or it is played mainly with the right hand, while the left hand damps the strings or plucks them in technically difficult passages. A later modification is the *cheng*, a favourite for solo and orchestral performances. It is played in a similar way as the *shê*, but plucked with the fingers of the right hand, whilst the left hand presses the strings down beyond the bridge to raise the sound by a half-tone or even more and to provide a vibrato.

European organology knows the *tsisiantsin (qixianqin, yangqin)* under the shortened name *ch'in (kin)*, but the fact that *kin* means, above all, a string instrument and that many Chinese musical instruments contain the word *kin* in their name, may cause misunderstandings. The invention of the *tsisiantsin* is ascribed to the Emperor Fu si. Written records exist as early as the sixth century BC. The shape of the *tsisiantsin* to this day recalls that it was made by splitting bamboo tubes lengthwise. All its parts are related to the cosmos: it measures three feet, six inches and six lines. This measurement symbolically recalls the 366 days of the year. It is six inches

MEMBRANOPHONES

CHORDOPHONES

wide, because there are six cardinal points: north, south, east, west, zenith and nadir. The small *tsisiantsin* has five strings, because there are five main tones. Across the centre it measures four inches recalling the four seasons of the year. The headpiece is wider than the base to indicate that what is noble is superior to what is low. Its top is convex like the sky, and its back flat like the earth. It has twelve basic *lü* and a supplementary octave, which together amount to thirteen. The strings run from two studs to pegs placed in the lower part of the headpiece. Each of the silk strings is made of a certain number of threads, the thinnest of forty-eight, the second of fifty-four, the third of sixty-four, the fourth of seventy-two, the fifth of eighty-one the sixth of ninety-six and the seventh and last string of 108 threads. It is not difficult to guess that the number relationship from the fifth string upwards corresponds to the tuning of the pentatonic scale. This means that two different and contradictory methods of tuning have been used on one and the same instrument. However, sound and acoustic laws must give way, since both methods of tuning are cosmologically accounted for. The tuning of the *tsisiantsin* depends on the scale in which the composition to be performed is written. The strings are most often tuned to D, C, F, G, A, c, d.

From the third century, closer contacts were formed between China and her western neighbours, permitting the import of musical instruments from India and Central Asia. It was probably then that the lute came to China from Central Asia. Known under the name *p'ip'a* it is today the most widely spread solo instrument not only in central and southern China, but also in neighbouring Korea, Vietnam, Cambodia and Japan. According to legend the Emperor Wu ti of the Wey dynasty had it made to recall three powers: heaven, earth and man, and five elements: fire, metal, wood, water and earth. The *p'ip'a* has a shallow pear-shaped body, gradually narrowing into the neck and terminating in the peg-box. The four strings are tuned according to the mode of the compositions played, mostly, a, d¹, e¹, a¹.

Another type of lute is the *hu le* or *ta hu le*, and the *sanhsien* (*sansjan, sanshyan*) which spread at the time of the Ching dynasty (221—207 BC) among the frontier garrisons of northern China. As the name of the instrument indicates *(san =* three, *hsien =* string) this is an instrument with three strings, with small, square or rectangular frame body of redwood, snakeskin belly and back. The long thin neck carries

Dance and instrumental ensemble of Vice-Regent Chang-ji-Chao. Bottom to top: drum *tang-pu*, lute *p'ip'a*, drum *changu*, reed *kuan*, flute *ti*, drum *po fu*, mouth-organ *sheng*, harp *kunghou*, clapper *pai pan*, drum *tang-ku*. After the wall painting from the cave temples in Tung-Chuang (Kan-su Province) from the Tchang dynasty (618—906)

a pegbox. Today it is made in two sizes. The larger is called *shuhsien (shusyan, sho-sen)* or *dagu sanhsien* tuned D, a, d, a, and together with the drum *dagu (tao-ku)* it accompanies narration in the south. The smaller one si called *tsiuhsan (tsiuhsien, cjujsan)* and is played in accompaniment to narration where declamation interchanges with song and instrumental accompaniment. The *tsiuhsan* is tuned either d, a, d¹, or a, d, a¹. The *yüeh chin (yuehchin)* is a guitar-like instrument with a wooden circular body, low rib, short neck and sickle-shaped head. According to Chinese legend a man from the country, Shin, living in the reign of Empress Wu (684—705) found an instrument in a tomb, and since it was round like the moon he called it *yüeh chin* (moon chin). According to another legend a string instrument was found in the tomb of Juenhjen, one of the seven wise men of the Bamboo Wood, and was named after this great man. The fixed tone series of the *yüeh chin* is determined by nine frets, three of which are on the fingerboard and six on the soundboard. The strings are tuned a fifth apart, d, d—a, a.

In all classes of the population of town and countryside a bowed chordophone *erh-hu (er = two, hu = abbreviation of the word huching, hu kin, fiddle)* is a great favourite. It has a hexagonal, or octagonal body of hard wood. Only very exceptionally is it cylindrical in shape. It has a snakeskin belly. The neck is formed by a stick piercing the resonator, having at the other end a slightly turned head with two pegs placed one below the other, sagitally. Two strings run from the lower part of the stick piercing the resonator over a bone bridge to the pegs, which are grooved to simplify tuning. For quick retuning a metal holder in the shape of the letter S is used. One of its semicircles holds the neck, the other the strings. This limits the resounding part of the strings tuned to the fifth d, a. When playing, the player sits, resting the spike on his knee. The hair of the bow passes between the strings, and the fingers of the left hand touch (never press, since the *erh-hu* has no fingerboard) both strings at the same time.

In the northern musical dramatic genre, *banczycjan (bangtzytsian)*, in which song is accompanied by rhythmical beats of the wooden clapper *bangs (bangtz)* the main accompanying instrument is the *banhwu (bangu)* with two strings, today also used in ensembles. It differs from the *erh-hu* in that its body has the shape of a decapitated coconut covered with a thin piece of wood. It is tuned one octave higher than the *erh-hu*, i.e. d¹, a¹. Other bowed instruments are mostly variants of the *erh-hu* or *banhwu*, such as the *sihu* with two pairs of strings, or the *jinghu* with a cylindrical resonator. The *jehu* belongs to the same type as the *banhwu* which is played in the province Guandun, and the *tichyn (teqing, tikin)* dates from the time of the Ming dynasty (1368—1644). It is interesting that the name *tichyn* is used also by the Chinese for the European violin.

Among the wind instruments it is the panpipe *pai shiau* that has a very old tradition. Literary records date from as far back as the twelfth century. It has from fourteen to twenty-four pipes placed in a flat case in such a way that the top and bottom ends of the pipes protrude. The transverse flute *ti (di)* is said to have come to China from Central Asia during the reign of Emperor U Di (140—87 BC). Later two types of transverse flutes appeared: the large flute *dakhenchuj (dachenchuj)* and the small flute *sjaokhenchuj (sjaochenchuj)*. Today the flute *ti* is about 61—63 cm long and has nine fingerholes. The first hole is covered by a delicate bamboo membrane; the further six are fingerholes and through the last two holes a string is threaded from which the instrument is suspended. At many points the tube is strengthened by rings of thread. In existing instrumental ensembles of the theatres of the type *kuntsjuj (kuncjuj)* the flute *tsjujdi (cjujdi)* is used, which developed from the *dakhenchuj (dachenchuj)*. In the operas, *bangtzytsian*, another variant of the *ti*, is used. It is called *banti*. Both these instruments, the *tsjujdi* and the *banti*, are produced with two tunings, differing from one another only by a semi-tone. The range of the *tsjujdi* is a — b³, or a flat — b flat³ respectively. The *banti* is a fourth higher, i.e. d¹—e⁴, or d flat¹ — e flat⁴ respectively.

Somewhat later than the *p'ip'a* there appeared in China a double-reed instrument, *kuan*, with wooden, bamboo or lead pipe, both ends of which were strengthened with a lead ring. The eight fingerholes gave the chromatic scale, which is not used

Chinese shepherd boy with end-blown flute

AEROPHONES

15

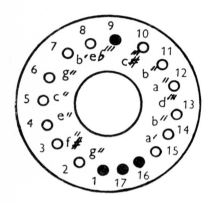

Cross-section of the Chinese mouth-organ *sheng*

Youth with mouth-organ *lushon*

in practice, despite the high technical level of play in which even complicated finger positions are used. The *kuan* is produced in various sizes, the most common being the *dakuan*, i.e. the large *kuan*, with a slightly conical tube and a range of e flat — a², and the *sjakuan*, i.e. the small *kuan* tuned a flat — c³. In the sixteenth century the Central Asian shawm reached China under the name *sona*. Similarly to the *kuan*, the *sona* also has eight fingerholes, but beyond that it has a conical tube. The double-reed terminates in a brass tube that often bears figural decorations. Before the reed is put into place, a copper or bone pirouette is put over the upper end of the head, serving as a lip rest. The *sona* is produced in two sizes: the large *sona*, *dasona*, tuned g flat — a flat², and the small *sona*, *sjasona* (also called *khajdi*, or *chajdi*) tuned c — a flat³.

The Book of Songs mentions the wind instrument *sheng* said to have been invented by Emperor Nyu-kwa in the third millenium BC. Records of it have been found in hieroglyphs engraved in bone from the time of the Yu dynasty (1401—1122 BC). The *sheng* was formed to imitate the shape of the Phoenix bird and it is probably under the influence of this tradition that it is being used to this day in China in funeral processions. It is usually made of seventeen bamboo pipes, their lower end showing a sloping cut. To this a metal free-reed of certain pitch is fitted. The lengths of the tubes are chosen to increase the sound of the reverberating tongue in the proper manner. The lower ends of the pipes are fitted into a common wind-chest with a mouthpiece. Just above the wind-chest, the pipes have holes that the player covers with his fingers. The reeds are set in motion both by inhalation and exhalation. The air stream passes through the opening and creates sub-pressure. Air then passes into the wind-chest and moves the reed to and fro. Sound is only produced if the lateral hole in the pipe is covered by the finger. If the hole is not covered, air will pass through it from the pipe without moving the reed. This is because the reed is less elastic than those of European mouth-organs. Thus by air pressure in the wind-chest, it is kept in a position permitting the air to escape without setting the reed in motion. But if the outer hole of the pipe is stopped, the pressure inside the pipe equalizes the pressure in the wind-chest and the reed is again able to close, so that the pipe speaks. If several holes are stopped simultaneously a chord is played. The *sheng* is the only Chinese instrument on which, apart from ditones in fourths and fifths, three, four and even more tones may be played at the same time.

The period of the Manchurian-Chinese dynasty (1663—1912) brought a decline in Chinese musical culture. The rulers of this epoch recognized and supported only the most ancient music, whereas they rejected the more highly developed instruments of more recent times. It was only the development of the classical theatre that helped some new musical instruments to penetrate. European musical instruments came to China first in the nineteenth century, causing many disputes among Chinese musicians. One group categorically refused everything coming from Europe, the other regarded Chinese instruments as primitive and outdated. Now there exist in China ensembles containing Chinese and European instruments side by side. No regulations exist which prevent the use of non-Chinese instruments, or the playing of music other than Chinese.

TIBET

Up to very recently music in Tibet was a secret protected from inquisitive foreigners with amazing vigilence. Foreigners were officially forbidden to enter the country; this law was applied fairly strictly, so that from the middle of last century few explorers succeeded in reaching Tibet. Conditions were extremely difficult for the courageous individuals who did manage to break through this bewitched circle and thorough and far-reaching investigations were impossible from the outset.

We know of the development of music in Tibet from the seventh century when the separate tribes united to form one state. As the result of very idiosyncratic living conditions, and the independent historical development of the country that had continued over a long period, a very characteristic way of life and customs developed. It is said that the people have as many songs and dances as there are mountain summits in Tibet. Music expanded as the result of two highly developed cultures, those of China and India. In no other country in the world does religion play so great a part in daily life as in Tibet and this is why temple and ceremonial music prevails. The Tibetans believe in Lamaism, which is a mixture of Buddhism and the original religion of the country — Bön. Due to the influence of Bön, Lamaism contains numerous shamanistic elements expressed in the ritual instruments of magicians and soothsayers. These instruments are often made from human bones. The rattle drum *rnga-chun*, in hour-glass shape, consists of two human skull-caps covered with skin. Cords with pellets are tied to the drum and if this is turned rapidly left or right they strike the heads. The trumpet *rkan-dung* is made of a human femur and covered with human or yak skin. It has a brass mouthpiece and may be adorned with corals or turquoises. Sometimes this trumpet has a wide brass flange on which are painted the three eyes and the nose of the demon that can be conjured up by the sound of this instrument.

The main ritual instrument of the Tibetan Lamas during service is the flat frame drum *lag-na*, set on a long wooden pole. It is beaten with a sickle-shaped stick fitted with a skin sphere. A pair of kettledrums with laced membranes are called *lda-man*. They are placed on the ground opposite each other, or suspended from the shoulders of the player in such a way that the drum with the lower tone hangs on his back and must therefore be played by another drummer. Artistically exquisite, ornamented instruments are included in the Horniman Museum collection in London. There is the temple shawm of Tibet, *rgya-glin*, with conical bore and an ornamented resonator of beaten metal; then a copper trumpet, *rkang-ling*, three metres long with tubular sections that telescope into one another. Sometimes this instrument is referred to as *cos-dung*. Then there is the marine-shell trumpet *dung* (or *dung-dkar*) made from the Xancus pyrum with mouthpiece and mountings of gold on copper, inlaid with corals and turquoises. Its deep sonorous sound is to be heard during funeral rites. The lute *pi-wang* has a hollowed-out wooden body. The sickle-shaped pegbox terminates in a carved animal head. A chordophone recalling the Indian *rebab* in shape is an unusual instrument. Its wooden body is covered with gold sheet artistically wrought and inlaid with semi-precious stones. It is not played with a bow but beaten with hammers like a dulcimer.

Tibetan folk music is closely linked with dancing and the theatre. The folk dance *tita* is accompanied by the six-string lute *ljusiancin (ljusyangquin)* or hemispheric brass bells *ma ling (malin)*. The instrumentalist stands with the line of dancers, dancing and playing simultaneously. When the bells are heard, the dancers start to sing and together with rhythmical stamping the sounds — *rita, tita* — begin, hence the name of the dance. The dance *ye (je)* is very popular in the southern part of the Sychuan pro-

Music for Tibetan oboes and drums

vince of China. This dance is named after the accompanying string instrument *ye*, which is very much like the Chinese violin *erh-hu*. The dance *zhöba*, regarded as a kind of prayer, is accompanied by the sounds of the tambourine. In the theatre of Tibet, where the actor's art consists mainly of singing and dancing, a large drum is used with a pair of copper cymbals, *sil-snyau*.

A special type of music found in Tibet is Sino-Mongolian, which is both secular and religious and very similar to the music of the Chinese provincial opera. Secular songs are accompanied on the transverse flute *dge-glie* or on the vertical flute *glin-bu*. Often two or three duct flutes are tied together to form a double or triple pipe. Another instrument used for accompaniment is the bowed instrument *kungka (kunghou)* with three strings. The sharp clanging sound in Sino-Mongolian religious music is provided by the miniature cymbals *tin-tin-sags*.

An important part of Tibetan music is made up of liturgical song which is accompanied by simple metallophones: a campaniform hand-bell called *dril-bu*, the triangular gong *bur rting* suspended from the chord of a wooden arch, or the gong chimes *tsang-chen* resembling the Chinese *yün lo*. To these instruments must be added the drums *chör na* and the trumpet *dung-chen* or *rkang-ling*. Apart from the above-mentioned instruments the bamboo Jew's harp *kapi* is known in Tibet, the small metal flute *prad-gling* and — to drive away evil spirits — the ram or antelope-horn *nva-dung*.

KOREA

The foundation for the musical culture of the Korean people was laid by the peasants' music *noniak*. Archeological finds have proved that from the earliest times clay whistle pipes *chun* and some idiophones were in use. In the ancient town of Choson, where music and dance celebrations were held annually, the string instruments *tengohangym* and *konchu* were used. It is a great pity that a considerable number of historical instruments preserved for centuries at the royal court in Seoul were lost during Japanese rule. Thus important material is lacking for a more thorough investigation of the development of musical instruments.

The basic tonal make-up of Korean music is the five-tone anhemitonic mode (without semi-tones) but a six and seven-tone system is also to be found. Of 107 musical instruments that once existed in Korea, according to the official assessment of Korean experts, only a mere sixty-seven have been preserved. These comprise thirty-five percussion, seventeen wind and fifteen string instruments. The greatest credit as far as the development of instrumental music and especially the production of musical instruments is concerned, must be given to the music reformer, composer, and instrument-maker Pak Yen, who worked under the Li dynasty in the fifteenth century. It was Pak Yen's task to revive Korean musical culture, then in a state of decline after exhausting wars. Pak Yen invented a notation, revived more than sixty types of musical instruments and, excellent theoretician that he was, investigated the specific features of the Korean folk music called *khanak (changak)*. On the basis of the results that he achieved he elaborated a new theory of music that went far to help revive the creative work of Korean composers.

As early as at the time of the Three States (Ist century BC — 7th century AD) records mention the pan-pipe *so*, which today consists of sixteen bamboo pipes of unequal length. The *sjan* or *sjanchvan (sanxian, sansian)*, consisting of seventeen bamboo pipes is the equivalent of the Chinese mouth-organ, *sheng*. The Korean flute *chettö* with seven fingerholes corresponds to the Chinese transverse flute *ti*. The vertical flute *tchunso* has six fingerholes. The shawm *sjanap* or *töpchenso* appeared first in Korea in the fifteenth century. It corresponds to the Chinese shawm *sona* and nowadays has a funnel-shaped metal resonator. In the folk ensemble the *sjanap* is the only instrument to carry the melody.

The considerable number of chordophones include two different types of harps, the *vagonchu* with thirteen diatonically tuned strings, and the frame harp *sugonchu* with twenty-one strings, known as early as the time of the Three States and identical with the Chinese harp *kunghou*. The Chinese guitar *ruan* is similar to the *volgym* (*volkum*) with four strings, and the Chinese lute *p'ip'a* corresponds to the lute *chjang-pipcha (xiangpipa)* with five strings. There are several kinds of zither which differ from their Chinese counterparts only in some minor constructional details. The invention of the *komungo* with six strings is ascribed to the musician Van San Ak who lived in the fifth century, the period of the Kogurjo. The favourite string instrument in Korea is the zither *kayagym* with thirteen strings, said to have been first built at the beginning of the sixth century by the musician U Ryk. The zither *kavjongum* also has thirteen strings, but they are of metal and the body is almost half the size of the *kayagym*. In appearance it resembles the bowed zither *djunadjan* with ten strings identical to the Chinese bowed zither *jezhang*. The dulcimer *yangum (yangym)* with a trapezoid body and larger number of metal strings recalls the Arab *santur*. The most widely used Korean violin *högym (höuhögum)* is derived from the Chinese instruments *erh-hu* and *jinghu*.

The big drum *sakko* is similar to the Chinese drum *kien gu*. It used to mark the beginning of the performance of a classic instrumental ensemble. It has an elongated wooden body and nailed skin membranes. The *sakko* is suspended from ornamentally carved wooden frames. The small drum *ryogo* is suspended at the same height as the *sakko*, but on a special stand with a central pole. Sometimes two or even three drums are to be found on the pole, one above the other. A larger drum with a low corpus and two nailed heads is called *buk*. The *sogo* is a small frame drum with a low corpus and short wooden handle. It is struck with a wooden mallet. A *dyango* is regarded as the typically Korean drum, shaped like an hour-glass but larger than the similar Japanese drum *ko-tsuzumi*. It appeared at the beginning of the Koryo period, (12th—13th century), in an ensemble consisting of more than two hundred musicians. This ensemble is regarded by the Koreans as the first large polyphonic ensemble in the history of music, which was imitated by other countries of the Far East. Today the body of the *dyango* is made of brightly lacquered metal. The heads are stretched with the aid of hoops and strong cords.

The Korean scraper *ö* is identical with the Chinese scraper *yü* of carved wood representing a crouching tiger on a plinth. The Chinese gong chime *yün lo* corresponds to the Korean *yunra* in construction and number of gongs. The most important instrument when village musicians are playing is the *kiangari*. A somewhat large gong, *din*, is used by village orchestras. Both gongs are suspended from cords and beaten with wooden mallets. A reform of musical instruments was recently carried out in Northern Korea with the aim of perfecting the technique of playing and in an effort to extend the tonal range of some of the instruments. The flutes *chettö*, *piri* and *sjanap* were fitted with a new key mechanism. The bodies of the bowed instruments *chögym* and *aden* were respectively reduced and extended in size. In the case of the zither *kayagym* not only was the body enlarged but the number of strings was also increased. The improved version of the *djunadjan* is made in three sizes, the *soadjan* (small), the *djunadjan* (medium) and the *tjöadjan* (large). These are further divided into bowed and plucked instruments.

The village ensemble, *nonak*, is made up of two gongs, *din*, three large drums, *bik*, two drums, *dyango (tanggu)*, a drum, *sogo*, a gong, *kiangari* and a mouth-organ, *sjan*. The efforts that are being made at present to revive traditional folk art and to perfect musical instruments indicate that Korean folk music is on the way to a new period of development.

Korean woman with drum *dyango*

JAPAN

The Japanese, as many other nations, have been great musicians for centuries. Historians have recorded that in the year 453 musicians from Korea came to Japan to perform during the Emperor's rites. This is also the year in which an orchestra of eighty musicians was first mentioned. From that time reports increased concerning the activities of foreign musicians coming to Japan from various parts of China, Turfan, Samarkand, South-East Asia, Korea and Manchuria. The Japanese, in turn, went abroad in search of musical education.

Very little of ancient Japanese music has been preserved. It is mainly the music of the *gagaku*, (which literally translated, means 'beautiful music') containing songs, dances and instrumental music. There is also *noh* music, which once used to be called *sarugaku* and since the second half of last century has been referred to as *nogaku*. To be exact, *noh* is not actually music, but a very special type of drama combining elements of song, dance, mime and instrumental accompaniment. *Nogaku*, cultivated since the second half of the fourteenth century by the Samurai, developed to become an art form used only by the ruling classes.

TONAL SYSTEM
The Japanese tonal system, derived from the Chinese, is based on natural forces, signs from heaven and the seasons. Since the laws of nature in Japan were always brought into context with the sacred number five, their musical theory is also based on the system of five tones. The pentatonic scales are arranged analogously to the modes used by the Chinese theoretician Lin-Len and are based on a series of rising fifths and falling fourths. The only difference between these two systems is that the Chinese and Japanese ascribe a different origin to the various parts of their theories and to their instruments. The Japanese use, beside the five basic tones, two more supplementary tones with signs that exist in Chinese theory, but that have never been used in practice.

In the eighth century a large orchestra was established at what was then the capital of Japan, Heian (the Kyoto of today) including seven kinds of wind, three kinds of string and seven kinds of percussion instruments. A dance called *gigaku*, which was much in favour and for which masks were used, was accompanied by an ensemble consisting of a flute *kagura* and drums *tsuzumi*. Instrumental music also accompanied the performances of jugglers and acrobats known as *sangaku* and *sarugaku*. All types of musical and dramatic art developed under the artistic influence of other Asian countries. When during the era of Heian (9th—12th century) these contacts were interrupted, a reform of the Japanese tonal system began and unsuitable instruments were eliminated. For three centuries music was provided for all ceremonial occasions by Japanese, Chinese and Korean musicians living in Heian. Music was regarded as an inseparable part of the education of any nobleman or member of the upper classes. A change took place in the twelfth century, when the army came to power. Formalist feudal music, linked mainly to courtly functions, disappeared and a new dramatic form composed of song recital and dance took its place. *Noh* drama up to the seventeenth century the prerogative of the ruling classes, is still alive today without any marked changes. The Emperor was permitted to have a small *gagaku* ensemble at his court in Kyoto. There the tradition of old court ceremonial continued, and *gagaku* grew in importance.

GAGAKU
Today the court ensemble *gagaku* holds a unique position in Japan. Members of this orchestra must learn to play one wind and one string instrument of the *gagaku*, and also one instrument used in a European symphony orchestra. The instruments of the orchestra include the oboe *hichiriki* and three types of the transverse bamboo flute *fuye*, i.e. the *o-teki* or *riu-teki*, the *koma fuye* and the *kagura*. The fingerholes of

20

the flute *fuye* are placed according to exact rules and its tones are the basis of vocal and instrumental music. A Japanese legend tells of a great flautist, Shioguen, who hid in a cave inhabited by a huge snake. When, at midnight, the snake appeared, Shioguen played a sad melody on his flute. The monster hearing the magic tones of the flute listened spellbound for a while and then departed without harming the terrified musician. Since that time it is believed that the sounds of the flute *fuye* drive away poisonous snakes. The mouth-organ *sho*, on which six tones may be played simultaneously, gives a characteristic timbre to the orchestra. The number of chords is limited to eleven by the structure of the instrument, but none are like any of the basic chords of the European three-tone system.

The lute *biwa (satsuma biwa)* was introduced to Japan by Satotogi in the ninth century during the reign of the Emperor Nimmio Tenno. A wide band of leather is fixed across the soundboard above the bridge. There are two crescent-shaped tone-holes. The four strings of the instrument are played with a plectrum and a special technique is used. The *biwa* is used more to give strong accentuation to the phrases than to lead the melody. The *biwa* of the court orchestra is called *bugaku-biwa*. In contrast to its smaller sisters from the island of Kyushu the *satsuma biwa* and the *chicuzen biwa*, it rests in a slanting position on the ground between the legs of the performer because of its great weight. The large drum *daiko (taiko)* accentuates every phrase. Opposite it stands the small bronze gong *shoko*, suspended from a circular frame on a stand. On particularly festive occasions the huge drum *da daiko* is used instead of the drum *tsuri daiko*. It is placed on a special raised platform surrounded by a gilded railing and decorated with colourful hangings. The drummer stands in front of it, resting his right leg on the first step of the platform so that he can strike it with all his force. The leader of the orchestra directs changes in tempo by means of the drum *kakko*, whose Korean name *kalko* stresses its affinity to barrel drums.

Apart from the above-mentioned instruments of the *gagaku*, the Japanese play on a three-stringed, long necked guitar *samisen*, which came to Japan from China in the sixteenth century and soon spread far and wide. Towards the end of that century there was a great *samisen* player, Ishimura Kengyo, of legendary fame. The *samisen* has a square body made of four pieces of wood covered with cat skin. The strings played with a big wooden plectrum, are tuned in five different ways. In the beginning the *samisen* was used to accompany popular songs; later, when the *samisen* began to be used also by the townspeople, the music named after it and played on it was relegated to the common people.

Japanese historians record that, under the reign of Emperor Ogin-Tenno, (AD 331) an old ship was broken up and its wood burned, and skilful Korean workers came to Japan and made a musical instrument called *koto* from the charred wood. Originally this instrument was used at court and called *so no koto*, later, under the name *koto*, it became a favourite folk instrument and was played in a different manner. Music schools teaching the *koto* developed a special style which reached its climax at the close of the seventeenth century. In structure and appearance the *koto* has much in common with the Chinese zither *tsisiantsin (yangqin)*. Its strings are divided into two groups containing three and four strings respectively. All strings have a common bridge and are played by plectra in the shape of long nails. The small bowed instrument *kokyu* resembles the Chinese *erh-hu*. Together with the *samisen* and the *koto* it often forms a chamber trio. The three lower strings of the *kokyu* are tuned in fourths and the two higher in unison.

Doo is the generic term for various kinds of gongs: the large bronze *tam tams*, the small *shoko* and the *dora (doraa)* of Korean origin. The surface of the *dora* is covered with small protuberances causing the upper tenth to dominate when it is beaten. Another Japanese xylophone is the *mokkin*, consisting of thirteen wooden slabs of differing length nailed to a felt belt resting on a wooden lacquered trough. The slabs are struck with two wooden mallets and produce the following amazing series of tones: d, e, f, a, c¹, d¹, f¹, g¹, b¹, c², d², e², f². The rattle *sudsu (suzu)* consists of a wooden handle and a base of five leaves. A metal wire is fixed to the base twisted into spirals to form concentric circles and twelve bronze bells are fixed to them. The clapper

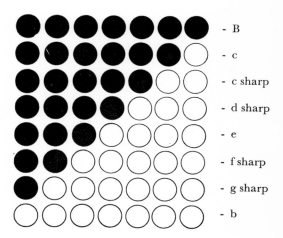

Touch system of the flute *fuye:*
● Finger on fingerholes
○ Fingerholes open

- B
- c
- c sharp
- d sharp
- e
- f sharp
- g sharp
- b

Playing the Japanese flute *fuye*. After the original in the Musée Cornuschi

Japanese drum *taiko*, drums *ko-tsuzumi* and *o-tsuzumi*, flute *fuye*. Woodcut 1805. Horniman Museum, London

shaku byoshi, the moon-shaped guitar *gekkin* and the panpipe *siao (hsiao)* are variations of the Chinese types as with most other Japanese musical instruments.

The last great flourish of Japanese music, quite idiosyncratic and uninfluenced by any outside factors, occurred during the period of Japanese isolation lasting until the succession to the throne of Emperor Meiji in the year 1868. After the proclamation of a constitutional monarchy Emperor Meiji chose to reside in Tokio where the tradition of the court of Kyoto was continued but nevertheless the Emperor's court adapted itself more and more to European models. Under the influence of western civilization Japanese music no longer expressed national art as it had for so many centuries. The office responsible for imperial court music ordered members of the court orchestra to study and perform European music as well as original Japanese music. Today Europeans teach at the conservatories. Classical Japanese music survives mainly in temples, theatres and private life. Since the end of the Second World War, when Japan was flooded with western dance music, even Japanese folk music has been strongly influenced by European music.

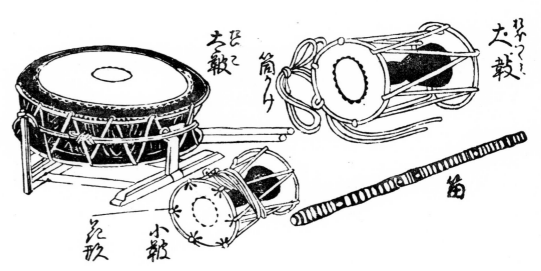

MONGOLIA

The thirteenth-century 'Secret Chronicle of the Mongolians', and reports of European ambassadors to the Mongolian court mention a specific Mongolian folk art in which the *morin khuur* was used; this is the musical instrument most widely in use in Mongolia to this day. The kettledrum *kurga (ko'urge)* was covered with the skin of a black bull and — since it was the symbol of power — the moguls used it to direct their battles. After the decline of the empire of Genghis Khan the Mongols returned to their old home, the steppe regions of Inner and Outer Mongolia, and to their old nomadic life. In the sixteenth century they accepted Tibetan Lamaism and with it the ritual music played in the monasteries. The monks, wandering from place to place with the musicians and performing their songs during celebrations and in military camps, became the bearers of traditional Mongolian music.

Musical instruments depicted in the frescoes of the temple in Erdenidzhu and the drum in the hands of the Indian priest Mahasiddha, painted on canvas demonstrate Chinese and Indian influence. Modern Mongolian folk songs are based on the pentatonic scale and monophony. A solo singer sings accompanied by the *khuur chi* or the *morin khuur*. The corpus of this trapezoid bowed chordophone with low wooden ribs and parchment tables recalls the Arabic *rabob*. Two horse-hair strings are tuned to the fifth. The *khuuchir* with a hexagonal or cylindrical soundboard covered with skin has four strings and fully corresponds to the Chinese bowed chordophone *erh-hu*. Mongolian folk music also makes use of a three-stringed chordophone *shanzu (shandze)* and a dulcimer *yochin* struck with two mallets. The *yatga (yatag)* with fourteen strings, plucked with the fingers, corresponds to the Chinese zither *tsisiantsin (yangqin)*. The flute *limba* is used both for accompaniment and as a solo instrument and corresponds to the flute *ti*, the gong chime *dudaram* is used in the same way. During Lamaistic rites the *temür-khuur*, the stirrup-shaped Jew's harp of the Mongols is used. The double *damaru*, the *shaman* flat drum with a handle which is still in use at the monastery of Erdeni-dzhu for musical performances and during prayers, the cymbals, the shawm *bishur* and the long trumpet *buri* come originally from Tibet. The development of Mongolian music in more recent times is closely connected with the progress of the music theatre founded in 1931 and the formation of an orchestra of folk instruments.

1

1. Heavenly nymph with cymbals

2. Ensemble of musicians in Paradise Pao-en-Sutra

3. Chinese gong chime *yün lo*

3

4

5

6

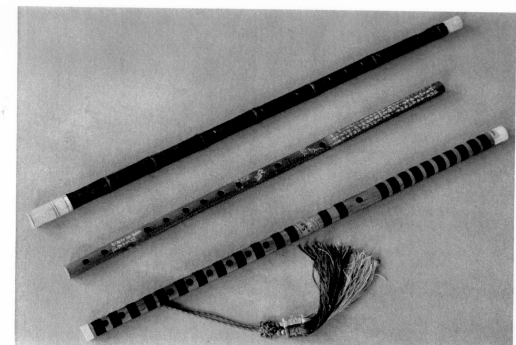

7

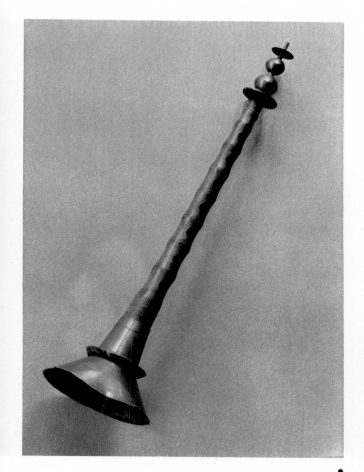

8

9

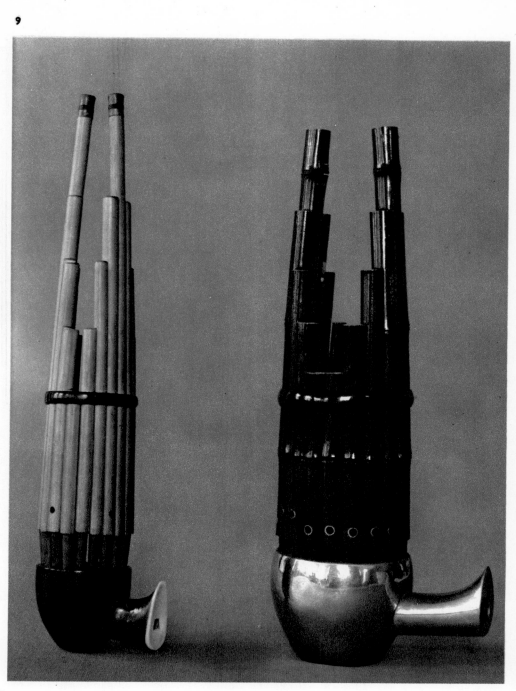

10. Chinese statuette with mouth-organ *sheng*

11. Chinese woman with lute *p'ip'a*

12. Zither
13. Playing the Chinese zither

14

14. Chinese dance with guitar *ruan*

15. Mouth-organ *lushon* and dulcimer *yangchin*

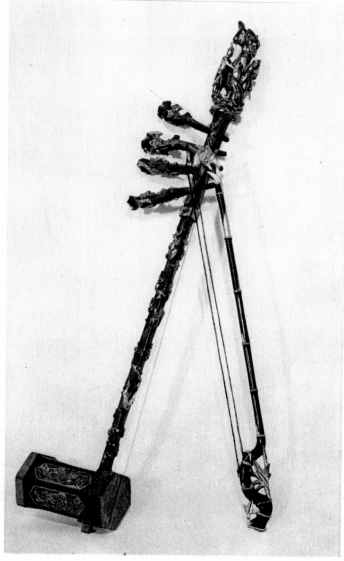

16

17

16.—17. Chinese violin *erh-hu* and detail of scroll

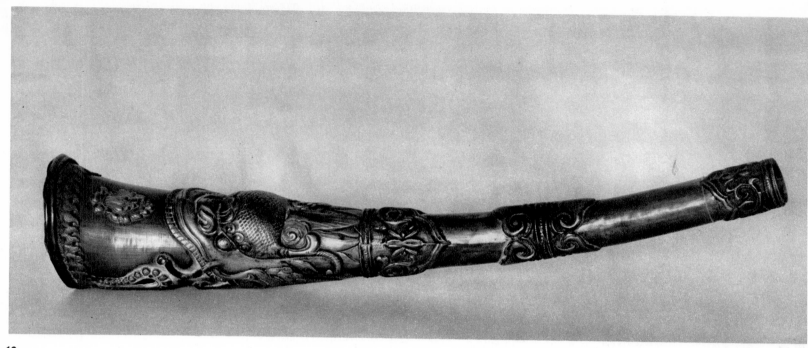

19

20

18. Ensemble of Chinese musicians

19. Tibetan horn *rkang-ling*

20. Tibetan percussion chordophone

21.—22. Ensemble of folk musicians in Lhasa

21

22

23

23. Tibetan trumpets *rag-dung*

24

24. Ensemble of Tibetan musicians

25. Tibetan musician playing the lute *pi-wang*

26.—27. Tibetan violin *kungka* and detail during performance

25

26

27

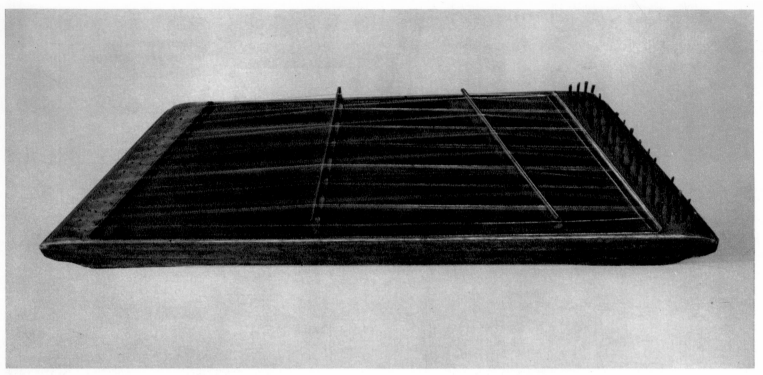

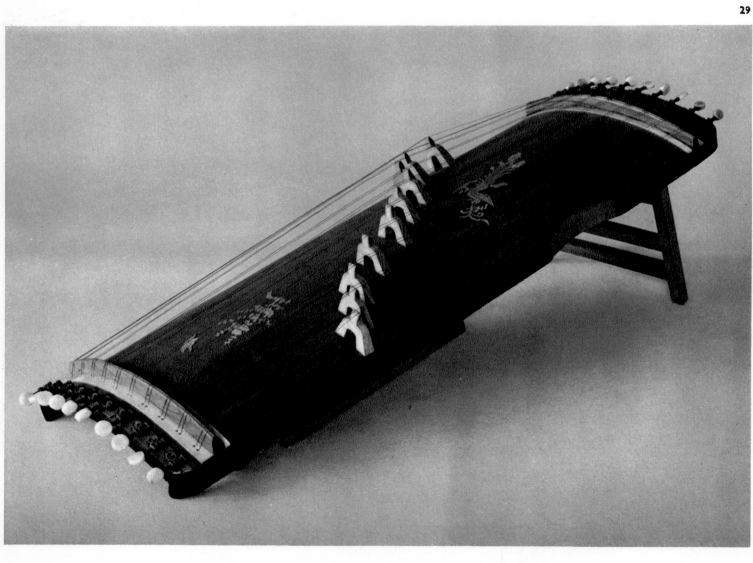

28. Korean dulcimer *yangum*

29. Korean zither *djunadjan*

30. Performance on the *kayagym*

31. Performance on the Japanese zither *koto*

32. Japanese instruments *koto* and *wagon*

33. Performance on the Japanese guitar *samisen*

34. Guitar *samisen* with plectrum

33

34

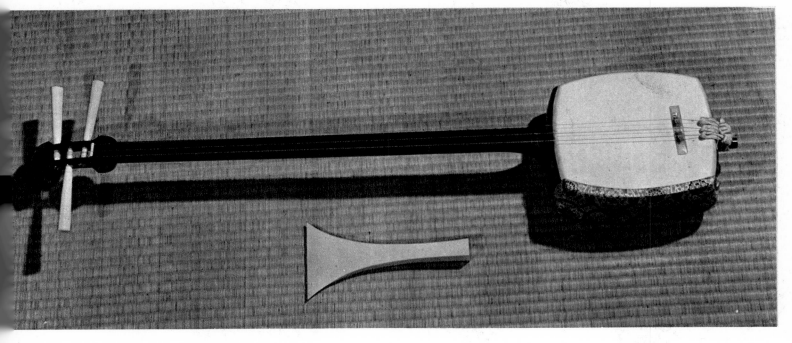

35. Member of the ensemble Gagaku with end-blown flute *shakuhachi*

36. Court player with drum *ko-tsuzumi*

37. Musicians of the court ensemble of Gagaku

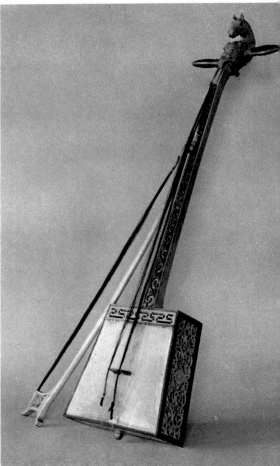

38. Mongolian street musician with *morin khuur*

39. Mongolian trumpet *rkan-dung*

40. Mongolian *morin khuur*

SOUTHERN ASIA

INDIA AND KASHMIR

At the turn of the third and the second millenium BC, Hindustan was inhabited by a gifted people, the Hindus, skilled craftsmen, who exchanged their goods with those of other countries. Trade routes led via the Caspian and the Black Sea to Europe. Exchange took place not only in the field of material goods, but also in science, literature and art. The ruins of the University in Taxila are proof of the existence of this once mighty cultural centre attended by young people from distant lands. When, at the beginning of the eighth century, the Arabs subjugated Persia, they also occupied part of India. Due to their influence Islamic culture penetrated the country. Regular contact with China, Greece, Iran and Central Asia enriched Indian culture and simultaneously made it accessible to other countries.

Since ancient times Indian culture has had its own tonal system, created its own national forms of song and dance, and its own musical instruments. Indians have no opera or symphonic music, but their songs and dances, often very complicated and elaborate, conceal limitless possibilities for further development. The foundations of the Indian tonal system were laid in ancient treatises devoted to problems of art and literature. The word 'sound' — 'nada' — is determined not only physically but philosophically. Every tone was ascribed a certain effect on the feeling and the consciousness of man. The Indian tonal system is based on a seven-tone diatonic series divided into seven main tones called *svara* and expressed by letters of the Sanskrit alphabet. This is the basic formation of Indian diatonics named after the syllables *sa-grama*. The tones of the main Indian scale are again divided into two, three, or four quarter tones called *shruti* (from the Sanskrit word *shru* = to hear, to differentiate) so that one octave extends over twenty-one *shrutis*. A large number of scales can be achieved from the basic scales by raising or lowering many tones. By combining different tetrachords Indian musicologists arrived at an astronomic figure — 34848 scales. In practice only the ten main scales called *raga* are used.

The *raga* is a certain melodious tune whose importance as an idiosyncratic form of creation is fundamental for Indian music. No researcher or musician interested in Eastern music can afford to ignore the Indian *raga*, whose fame in its heyday spread from the banks of the Ganges to the cities of Spain. Indian scholars and writers, beginning with Bharata, Matangi and Shrangavedi and finishing with contemporary investigators, have paid great attention to the *ragas*. Even though each of them has his own personal view on the basis of the *raga*, all agree that it has an aesthetic effect on man. The melodies of the *raga* seem to embody the complicated world of ethical, aesthetic, religious and philosophic views. Magic powers are ascribed to the *ragas*. They are supposed to be able to calm the raging elements, tame wild animals, conjure up fruits from the earth. Oriental fantasy made living beings out of the *ragas* and in India they are even depicted. One such picture shows a young warrior holding in one hand the head of his beheaded enemy, in the other a drawn sword, and at the same time listening to the song of two maidens. The *raga* can only develop to its full effect if played at the correct and strictly limited time. No Indian musician would dare play a melody in the evening which belongs to an afternoon *raga*, though often the day *raga* differs from the evening *raga* only by the raising of one single tone in the melody.

TONAL SYSTEM

The seven main tones of the Indian scale

Indian *raga mallar*

The origin of musical instruments, as with the origin of everything, is ascribed by Indians to the gods. The gods invented them, the gods played on them, the gods enjoyed the songs of the heavenly singers and musicians — the *kinnaras* and *gandharvas*. The god Shiva who by his dance could destroy and create worlds, was sometimes accompanied by an orchestra that did not and never will have an equal: its players were the senior gods of the Hindu pantheon. Sarasvati, Brahma's wife, played the *vina*, Indra the flute, Brahma the cymbals measuring time, Vishnu the drum and Lakshmi sang. Aesthetically instrumental music has always been assessed very highly in India. The treatise *Sangita-ratnakara* states that playing an instrument gives man energy, develops his feelings and courage, touches his heart and drives away evil and bad qualities. Inventiveness and skilful hands have produced a treasury of instruments in India famed far beyond the frontiers. Many have passed the test of centuries, but some were found wanting and soon fell into disuse, as if they had failed to adapt themselves to the changes occuring from time to time in the style of Indian music. Others were perfected and have become classic instruments of modern time.

Bharata, in his classification of musical instruments into four groups, preceded the Hornbostel-Sachs system by many centuries. He calls string instruments 'taut' *(tata)*, idiophones 'fixed' *(ghana)*, membranophones 'covered' *(avanaddha)* and wind instruments 'perforated' *(susira)*. It is very difficult to record Indian names for musical instruments, since they differ in each of the many Indian languages.

Bronze cymbals are used in south India as the rhythmical accompaniment of folk music and in north India for ritual music. Their origin is ascribed by Indian mythology to the spirit Ravana and the sirens Kinnara. The larger cymbals *jhanja* are similar to the Turkish cymbals. They have a wide flat rim, central boss and are connected pairwise by a cord threaded through their centre. The player clashes the cymbals at various angles and in varying manners; from the outside, the inside, at the edges, and thus gives the sound of the *jhanja* different timbres. Thick-walled cup-shaped cymbals are called *tala* (also *mandira*). Unlike the *jhanja* they are not connected by a cord, but are fitted with a tassle that serves as handle. When clashed they emit a high tinkling sound like bells. The *kurtar* or *chittika* is a clapper consisting either of small bells or pieces of wood suspended from two wooden frames. These are held in one hand and clicked together by an opening and closing movement of the fingers. An unusual, but for India typical, instrument is the *ghata (ghatam)*, a percussion pot resembling a pottery jar, the opening of which is pressed against the player's bare stomach. The rhythm is tapped out by the fingers on the corpus of the instrument. Eighteen porcelain dishes arranged into a semi-circle form the *jaltarang*. The player strikes the dishes — carefully tuned by the amount of water they contain — with bamboo sticks.

Perhaps no other advanced culture has developed as perfect a system of rhythms in its music as Indian culture. A suitable contrast to the modal character of Indian music was formed — apart from idiophones — by the sensitive playing technique of the drums. Indian drums are mostly struck with the hands and fingers and not by sticks, permitting a wide variation of technique. Every strike is named according to whether is made by the left or the right hand, or by both together, or whether the fingers or the palms are used. The *mridanga* (also called *mathala, matalam)* is a double-membraned wooden drum of elongated barrel shape, according to legend invented by Brahma himself. The centre of the smaller membrane is smeared with a paste of resin, oil and wax or a layer of dough made from wheat flour to give the drum a deeper tone. The *mridanga* of the north is more decorative than that of the south which has more stretching thongs. In the north preference is given to two or more smaller drums of Arabic origin called *tabla*. Usually this is a pair of drums of different size tuned as the *mridanga*. Sometimes another small kettle-drum, *bahya (baya)* is added. If a larger number of *bahyas* are used in one performance they are tuned to permit the playing of a melody. The old Indian-style *dhrupad* requires a cylindrical double-membraned drum *pakhawaj*, similar to the drum *mridanga* but with a much stronger sound.

During official ceremonies, in processions and at temples the kettle-drum *nagara* (sometimes also called *bheri* or *nakkera*, from the Persian-Arabic *naqqara)* is used.

It has a welded corpus of copper or iron. In Ramahyana and Magabharat it is also called *dundubhi*. In the palace ensembles huge kettle-drums, *mahanagara* or *nahabat* are used. They have a diameter of up to 180 cm and are carried by elephants. The player sits on the frame of the drum and strikes it with two bent sticks. A pair of small copper kettle-drums *sutri nahabat* are mounted on a camel. Folk ensembles use a drum *dhola* with a one-piece corpus. Women play on a smaller *dhol* called *dholki*. *Dholuk* and *dak* are drums similar to the *dhol*. Their shape varies from region to region. Magicians use a miniature drum in the shape of an hour-glass, called *budbudika* (or *budubuduke*). A cord, with leather or cork pellets on the ends which strike against the head when the drum is shaken, is wound round the centre.

Tambourines include the *daff* or *daffde*. These sometimes measure more than one metre in diameter and are played with the fingers of the right hand and a thin bamboo stick held in the left. The smaller single-membraned drum *daira (daera)* is played in a similar way. The thumb of the left hand is placed in a slit in the bottom part of the instrument thus forming a support for the left hand so that the joint of the middle finger can press the skin if the tone is to be raised. A large instrument of this kind from south India is called *tambattam (thambatte)*. Its diameter may reach as much as 150 cm. Folk tambourines are represented by the *kandjeri (kandzeri)*. Rattling discs are fitted into three or four openings in its frame. The membrane of fine calf parchment or skin is tuned by moistening.

Wind instruments have changed very little in the course of thousands of years. Many of them are similar to those found in other countries, but they have attained inimitable national features in India. This is true above all for the bamboo cross flute *murali* or *pillagovi*. Archeological finds have confirmed that the flute was known in India before the coming of the Aryans. It seems that in the beginning it was not as popular among the Aryans as the *vina* and the drums, since these two instruments are mentioned far more frequently than the flute in early Indian literature. Nevertheless, the flute was and is a very popular instrument. It can be heard in towns and villages, in private homes and in the concert hall. Krishna himself played on the flute when he hid in a shepherd's house to escape death. The *murali* has six and sometimes seven

AEROPHONES

Indian street musicians with drums and copper horn *ranasringa*

fingerholes, playing a sharp[1], b flat[1], b[1], c[2], d flat[2], e flat[2], f[2]. Apart from the cross flute there are a whole number of instruments originally played only by the country people. One of these is the whistle flute with a small resonator and pleasing sound. The *algosa (algosa, alguoji)* is a kind of flageolet with the same tone range as the *murali*. In the north and in the Punjab it has developed into a double flute.

During wedding ceremonies and processions the penetrating sounds of the shawm or oboe, *surnai* or *shanai* of Arabic origin, are often heard. A drone is provided by blocking all the fingerholes but one in the second instrument with wax. In the south the *shanai* corresponds to the *nagasuram (nagasvaram)* with a conical bore terminating in a metal bell. Out of the twelve holes only seven are fingerholes, the others are blocked with wax and are tuning holes. This instrument is very difficult to play and requires long training. It is possibly for this reason that playing the *nagasuram* has become the traditional prerogative of certain castes where the art is passed from father to son. The *mukavina* is similar to the *nagasuram*, though it is about half its size. It has seven fingerholes according to the intervals of some scale and a high-pitched squealing sound. The *tubri (tumeri, pungi, pingivi, jinagovi)* is found throughout India. Used by the snake charmers, the two parallel pipes are made of cane, with the mouthpiece end inserted into a globular gourd or a calabash serving as wind chamber. The right pipe is the melody pipe and has seven or eight fingerholes. The left pipe is a drone. The *tubri* is used in the *raga nagavarali* which is supposed to please the snakes. India is the home of the bagpipe. The *shruti upanga* or *bhazana shruti*, with one reed pipe and a bag of kid skin, is the bagpipe of southern India. It is blown through a small mouthpiece. The vibrating reed made from thin reed or larger swamp grasses can be regulated by a small length of wire or fine thread twisted round it. In northern India and Kashmir a bass pipe is added and such a bagpipe is then called *moshug (moshuk, mashak)*.

The marine shell trumpet *sankhu* is one of the oldest wind instruments existing in India. There are reliefs, dating from the second century BC, depicting the trumpet in the temple at Bharata. The *sankhu* is a purely ritual instrument, played in front of the altars of Hindu gods. The use of the *ranasringa (ranashringa, sringa, sing)*, which was once made of buffalo horn, is more widespread. It is a crescent or S-shaped metal trumpet made of several curved brass sections that fit into one another. In the past no important person set out on a journey without having one or more *ranasringa* players in his entourage. When the party approached a town or village, the trumpeters announced their arrival by fanfares. The *ranasringas* answered from the gates of the town and it often happened that the trumpeters of both sides tried to outdo one another. On festive occasions Brahmins or priests play the *kurna (karna)* in the temples. This is the straight ceremonial trumpet of India, which also marks the players' high rank.

Indian musicians with copper horns *ranasringa*

CHORDOPHONES

The most important place among string instruments is held by the *vina*, which is beloved by everyone. According to legend it was formed by Shiva, who took inspiration from the sight of the lovely, resting Parvati. Her beautiful ivory breasts rose and fell rhythmically, her arms adorned with bracelets also recalled music. Shiva was intoxicated by this sight which remained engraved on his memory for ever. He had no peace until he succeeded in embodying this image in a musical instrument. The *vina's* long neck represents Parvati's slender figure, two gourds her perfect breasts, the metal frets her bracelets and the sound her rhythmical breathing. The *vina* with two gourds first appeared in the fifteenth century. In northern India, where it is played to this day, it is called *bin*. The many variations of the *vina* differ only slightly from one another in construction, but all have the long wide neck forming the instrument's main axis and a large number of frets and resonators. The *vina* is a very highly decorated instrument, usually beautifully carved and adorned with gold, silver and ivory. It has been depicted in stone and recorded by the painter's brush in charming miniatures.

The *bin* has four strings stretched over the frets and tuned D, A, e, c sharp[1] or G, a, c[1], f[1]. Two of the three remaining strings are led along the left side of the fingerboard and tuned a[1], a or c[2], c[1], and the third string on the right is tuned A or E (A) according to what *raga* is being played. One of the gourds rests on the player's left shoulder, the other against his right knee. The strings are plucked with a metal plectrum held by two fingers of the left hand, the little finger plucks the strings on the left side. The construction of the *rudra vina* is somewhat more complicated. The lower gourd is replaced by a piriform wooden resonator and the upper gourd is smaller. Four of the seven strings run over the fingerboard and the other three along the left side of the neck. The strings are tuned in three ways: 1) G, c, g, e^1, e^1, g^1, c^2; 2) G, d, g, d^1, d^1, g^1, d^2; 3) F, c, f, e^1, e^1, f^1, c^2. The steel, brass or silver strings used are specially produced for *vinas* in Channapatna and Mysore or in Bareilla in the north. The production process is secret and in the hands of a special caste. The *rudra vina* is either held in the same way as a *bin* or the player sits cross-legged on the ground holding it in his lap. The strings are never plucked with a plectrum but only with the player's long nails.

In appearance the northern *vina* is very like the *bin-sitar* with removable frets arranged as the frets of the *sitar*. The *tayus* also has removable frets. This instrument is also called *esrar* or *mohur*. Its resonator is shaped like a peacock and it has drone strings. Another type of *vina* called *vichitra vina* in the north of India (sometimes also *bicitrabin*) and *gotuvadyam* in the south, has no frets. The strings are plucked with a metal plectrum and simultaneously rubbed with a small wooden cylinder or a piece of smoothly polished glass. There is a type of *vina* common in southern Kanara and Mysore whose name *kinnari (kinnari vina)* recalls the biblical instrument *kinnor*. It has three gourd resonators and twelve frets. Of the two or three wire strings one is led high above the frets and tuned a fourth or fifth lower than the other strings.

The bowed chordophone *sarangi* is regarded as the Indian violin. The corpus is made from hollowed-out wood with a waisted belly covered with parchment. The neck is short and wide to accommodate three (sometimes four) catgut strings tuned to c, g, c^1, (the fourth string to d) and about fifteen metal drone strings, tuned chromatically. The bow, consisting of a simple stick without frog and horsehair, is slightly curved. Though the sound of the *sarangi* is full and very pleasant, it is looked down upon by the higher castes, since it was formerly the instrument of the dancer-prostitutes. It is now used by lower-caste musicians or Muslims as accompaniment to theatre performances or in dance orchestras. In northern India nad Pakistan the *sarangi* is more highly decorated, with the head carved in the shape of a swan. The back of the instrument is rounded and the number of drone strings lower. A smaller type of *sarangi* is called *chikara* in Bengal. Three horsehair or catgut strings are tuned like the *sarangi* or to c, f^1, g^1, and five drone strings are tuned to G, B, A, d, e.

A type of *sarangi* called *sarinda* is a very common folk instrument not only in Bengal but also in Pakistan and Afghanistan. It is narrower than the *sarangi* and the belly is not covered by parchment but remains open. Three catgut or silk strings are tuned to g, —c^1, c^1. A very simple folk instrument, the *ravanatta*, is found throughout the East, it consists of a bamboo stick and a coconut shell covered with skin. Bells are fixed to the bow which is tied to the instrument by a cord. When played the bow passes between the two strings that are stretched, not side by side, but one above the other. Sometimes the *ravanatta* has three strings and several drone strings.

Kashmir, situated on either side of the upper reaches of the Indus and wedged between China and Pakistan, has a rich musical tradition. The *Radzha tarangini* chronicle of the twelfth century states that the most famous musicians of their time congregated at the court of the Emperors Dzhalok and Lalitaditia. The Muslim administrators of the country also supported music in Kashmir. In the fifteenth century, Sultan Zajnal Abidin used to hold music festivals to which he invited musicians from many countries. He was himself an excellent singer. There is no solo singing in Kashmir. All melodies are sung by a choir with instrumental accompaniment. The classical music of Kashmir, *sufianu kalam*, is accompanied by the dulcimer *santur* (hundred strings), a descendant of the Persian-Arabic instrument *kanun* (*qanun*). According to legend the first *santur* was made by the philosopher Katyayana, which accounts for its name *katyayana-vina* (in Sanscrit also *shatatantri*, which means hundred strings). It has a hundred metal strings and a trapezoid corpus. It is played with two light wooden beaters shaped like hockey sticks. Its sounds fill in the pauses between different parts of texts.

The most popular of all musical forms is the *chakkri*. The singers tune their instru-

KASHMIR

Drummer from Ceylon

ments and sing a previously unprepared and unrehearsed song. The main singer reads the verses and the choir catches the chorus spontaneously. Instruments used for the *chakkri* stress rhythm above all and therefore consist mainly of percussion instruments and the clay drums *not* or *tumbakhnari* with small bells attached to the ribbon. If these instruments are lacking they are easily replaced by a bunch of keys. The drum *not* is included in the ensemble even if there is a *rebab* or *sarangi*. In recent times this drum has been made more and more frequently from bronze. An important part is played by the goblet drum *tumbakhnari (zangskar)* held under the player's arm and beaten with both hands. The *tumbak*, widespread among country dancers, is similar to the *tumbakhnari*. Apart from the transverse flute *zanskar* the *rebab* is now being more and more frequently used as a solo instrument in the *chakkri* ensemble. This is a plucked instrument of Afghan origin recalling the Indian *sarod*. The metal sounding stick, a speciality of Kashmir, is used in the manner of the Greek lyre of Homeric times. It accompanies the inimitable songs *ladi shah* sung by minstrels wandering from village to village during harvest time.

PAKISTAN

The musical culture of Pakistan has developed side by side with the musical culture of India for thousands of years and bears all the marks of this coexistence. The great cultural centres of the Ancient East with their famous buildings have been of great influence in its formation. The folk *ragas* are a popular kind of Pakistani musical creation which vary greatly both in composition and content. They are performed at special times of the year and there exists no Pakistani musician who would play a spring *raga* in the winter months.

Musical instruments are not only intended as accompaniment to songs and dances but also for solo performances. Of the large number of instruments, most of which are identical with their Indian counterparts, the chordophone *sitar*, much used in India, has preserved its original shape and timbre. The story goes that it was invented by the great musician Amir Chusrau (Amur Khusru) who lived in the thirteenth century at the court of Sultan Alauddin Khildzhi in Delhi. The corpus of the *sitar* is made of hollowed-out wood or a gourd and has a wooden belly. The long neck carries a wide fingerboard with eighteen, or sometimes sixteen, elliptic metal frets secured to the fingerboard by springs passing under the bottom part of the neck to retain their mobility, as the frets are positioned for each required scale. Originally the *sitar* had three strings *(si =* three, *tar =* string), today it usually has seven, tuned to f^1, c^1, c^1, g, g^1, c^2, c^3. The *sitar* is plucked with a metal plectrum worn on the player's right forefinger. A *sitar* with ten to fourteen drone strings is called a *taraffedar*, a sitar with a flat corpus is called a *kachwar (kachwa, kachapi-wina)* and in Bengal a *surbahar.*

The *tambura* with four strings, used purely as accompaniment to song, is the inseparable companion of the wandering minstrels. The body is of wood with a slightly arched belly and small sound holes. The long unfretted neck has four pegs and the strings are never stopped but are gently plucked with the player's fingers. Strung beads, called *pusalu,* wedged between the belly and the strings serve to change the latter's pitch. Apart from the beads the *tambura* also has a *capotasto,* a movable nut, tied or clipped to the fingerboard, permitting the shortening of the speaking length of all the strings simultaneously. The basic tuning of the strings is G, g, g, d. The monochord *ektar* (Bengali *ekatantrika-*one string, also *tungtungi)* is the instrument of the mendicant monks. It is made from a bamboo stick with a gourd resonator or a hollow wooden cylinder fixed to the lower end. The open bucket-like body has a membrane of parchment at the bottom with a string passing through the centre. It is attached to the membrane with the help of a knot and passes to the top of the bamboo stick. The *ektar* is played by plucking the string gently to prevent the membrane from tearing, usually to the accompaniment of a drum, while the narrators hold a monotonous dialogue dealing with humdrum problems of the village or important persons who are present.

The Persian *sitar* is known in the Islamic world as the *kemanje (kemandzhe, kamanja)* i.e. bowed instrument. Today the Persian *sitar* is not played as frequently as in the past. It has often been depicted in the hands of noble persons on charming miniatures. It has a wooden corpus decorated with ivory and a parchment-covered belly. The three gut strings are tuned in the same way as the strings of the Indian *sarangi.* The *kanun (qanun,* from the old Greek word *kanon =* rule) or *svaramandalu (svaramandala),* rarely played now, is a zither instrument of Persian origin with trapezoid corpus. It usually has twenty-one steel strings plucked with two metal plectra worn on the finger tips. The *esrar (esraj, esradzh)* with a quiet and very pleasant sound combines elements of the *sitar* and the Indian *sarangi.* It was first made under Islamic rule when the women of the harem whiled away their time by singing. Since it was not possible

Indian singer accompanying himself on the *tambura*

that they should be accompanied by men and since most of the plucked chordophones were big and heavy, a smaller bowed instrument was made whose corpus was fashioned from a hollowed-out piece of wood and covered with parchment. Apart from five metal strings tuned to g, g^1, c^1, c^1, and f^1, it has ten to fifteen drone strings.

Indian music was always on a high level. It flourished at the court of princes, kings and Mogul rulers. The last Mogul ruler, Aurandzeb, a bigoted Muslim opposed to all forms of art, particularly music, was an exception. This was suffered with great difficulty by his subjects and they decided to soften his heart. They took bars, ranged themselves in a long procession, beat their breasts, tore their hair and with great lamentations passed slowly beneath the windows of the severe ruler. When he saw such deep sorrow and misery he was impressed and, asking what had happened, was told that the goddess of music had died, as too little appreciation had been shown to her, and that this was her funeral procession. 'Dig a deep grave' he was supposed to have shouted, 'so that no sound, no echo may be heard any more.' Fortunately the ruler's wish did not come true. Indian and Pakistani music is still alive.

AFGHANISTAN

Afghanistan is an inland state bordering on the Soviet Union in the north, Pakistan and China on the south and east and Iran on the west. The Afghans are first mentioned in the tenth and eleventh centuries. In ancient times and during the Middle Ages Afghanistan was ruled by the Persians, Mongols, Arabs and the Turks. It was only in the middle of the eighteenth century that an Afghan dynasty came to power. Afghans form more than half the population of the country. Tadzhiks, Uzbeks, and Turkmenians live in the regions bordering on the Soviet Union; there are also many, numerically very small, groups of other nationalities, and a large number of Mongols. Musical culture corresponds to the ethnological differences in the country. Mention is made of music in the earliest written records dating from the twelfth and thirteenth centuries.

Folk singers hold an important position in Afghan spiritual life. Every night the people assemble to gossip, sing and dance to the accompaniment of various musical instruments. In comparison with the unusually diverse development of Afghan music its armoury of instruments is somewhat simpler, made up mainly of instruments from the neighbouring countries, above all India.

The basic instruments of Afghan music are chordophones and membranophones. Most frequently used among the string instruments is the *tanbur* with frets and drone strings, which is plucked. The *rebab* with three pairs of melody strings and ten drone strings, and the *sarinda* with three strings, are indistinguishable from their Indian cousins, and the same is true of the bowed *dilruba (dilrubab)*. The rectangular *kemanje (kamanya)* with two strings is typical of the entire Middle East. The rhythm of Afghan music is supported by the drums that can be divided into two groups: single membrane instruments of Persian origin with a goblet-shaped corpus called *zerbaghali*, and double membrane instruments of Indian origin. Small cross flutes with two fingerholes are played during folk dances, prayers and funerals.

SOUTH-EAST ASIA

The music of South-East Asia played in Cambodia, Laos, Thailand, Burma and Vietnam differs from other Oriental music by its amazing tonal system, represented today by the music of percussion and string ensembles, the music of the mouth-organ *khen* of Laos and religious songs. This music, in the same way as Javanese music, uses polyphonic means to create a particular atmosphere and produces feeling by the complex creation of tones; the melody as such plays a subordinate part. The main bearers of this original musical tradition are instrumental ensembles including above all metallophones, xylophones, drums and wind instruments.

The great French sculptor Auguste Rodin once wrote about the court orchestra of Cambodia that it 'offers everything that used to exist in the classical age'. In the

Afghan musician playing the drum *zerbaghali*

CAMBODIA

59

recesses of the ruins of the grandiose twelfth-century Buddhist temple, Angkor Wat, there are statues of the dancers of Queen Apsaras. Their art is only meant for the eyes of the gods; ordinary mortals may only see their depictions . . . And suddenly these statues come to life. Apsaras descends to the ground, surrounded by her maidens and begins to dance on the square in front of the temple. This is the opening scene of a performance by the Royal Song and Dance Ensemble. Today three main types of musical art exist in Cambodia: folk music, religious music and classical music. Each of them has its own orchestra made up of a certain number of musical instruments of a certain type.

Two classical ensembles, the *pimpéat* and the *mohori* were formed in the sixteenth century (at the time of Bantéasy-Longvek). The *pimpéat* orchestra was named after the shawm *pey (sralay)* which is the leading instrument of the ensemble. Its tube is narrowed at both ends, it has a metal mouthpiece and a double reed. The other instruments of the orchestra include xylophones, gong chimes and drums. On particularly festive occasions the *pimpéat* is extended to include string instruments and is then called *mohori*.

The gong chime, *khong*, already depicted in the sculptures of the temple Angkor Wat, is known far beyond the frontiers of Cambodia and throughout the entire area of South-East Asia. It consists of sixteen tuned gongs arranged in a low semi-circular wooden frame. The player sits in the centre of the frame and strikes the gongs with two mallets, the ends of which are wrapped in elephant skin. The tone of the instrument is startlingly silvery, the deeper tones somewhat wavering. The *khong* is made in two sizes. The larger is called *khong tom* and has a tonal range of c^1—e^3. The smaller, *khong toch*, has a penetrating sound, range c^1—d^3.

In Europe the xylophone *ronéat* is mistakenly considered to be a typically Cambodian instrument, for it originated in India and came to Cambodia via Thailand in the nineteenth century. Three kinds of *ronéat* are used, all boat-shaped on a base. The *ronéat-ek* has twenty-one bamboo or wooden slabs and is very high-pitched. The *ronéat-thung* has sixteen slabs of lower pitch and the *ronéat-dek* has 21 metal slabs.

The *pimpéat* includes a pair of large barrel drums *skor-thom* whose heads are covered with buffalo skin. They are placed on a base in a slanting position. Their deep

Cambodian guitar *chapei*

tone recalls the European kettle-drum but they have no definite pitch. Another type of barrel drum, the *sampho*, comes from Malaya. Its corpus is made in one piece. Both heads, one of them of larger diameter than the other, are covered with calf skin. The instrument is placed horizontally before the player on a stand with two legs and tapped with both hands. Country players have a single membrane drum *romanea*, worn on a belt, akin to the elongated drum *skor-khayam* from Laos.

The first place among the string instruments is held by the very widely used plucked instrument *chapei*, recalling in shape the Mongolian *morin khuur*. It has a small flat trapezoid corpus and long neck. In the province of Kompong-Kham the neck is so long that the player can hardly reach the head. The two pairs of strings are tuned to the fifth. The zither *takhe*, with a corpus carved in the shape of a crocodile, is used in the *mohori* ensemble and to accompany song. It dates from the Angkor period when all its three strings, tuned A, e, a, were played. Today only two strings are plucked, by an ivory plectrum.

String instruments in Cambodia and Burma are called *tro (so* in Laos and Thailand). The types are distinguished as *tro-chei, tro-so* and *tro-khmer*. The oldest of them is the *tro-khmer* with three strings, similar to the Javanese *rebab*. It has an oval corpus with curved back, goatskin belly and long metal spike. The player stretches the hair of the bow by placing his fingers between the hair and the stick. This hampers the player so that he can hardly change the position of the bow. What the right hand cannot do must be done by the left. The left turns the instrument to place the required string against the unchangeable plane of the bow. Thus the left hand is forced to carry out two things in the course of play: it must lightly and quickly turn the neck of the instrument and the fingers must touch the frets with slight, quick and direct movements. To master the *tro-khmer* is so difficult that a normal staccato rouses the listeners' admiration and only very few elect can play arpeggio.

LAOS

No other Asian country reserves such an honourable position for women as Laos, and there are few countries where the people so constantly speak and sing of this fact. The songs are also remarkable since they are not merely solmisized as is the case in Vietnam, but actually consist of a series of chords. There is no doubt that as far as melody is concerned the music of Laos is indebted to that of Vietnam and Cambodia, but nevertheless it must be regarded as autochthonous as far as accompaniment on the *khen* is concerned, an instrument which is typical of Laos. This simple counterpart of the Chinese mouth-organ *sheng* is formed by bamboo pipes from one to three metres long. The pipes have gourd wind chests and free reeds that are set in motion by inhalation and exhalation, if the small hole in the respective pipe is stopped by the finger. When the *khen* is used to accompany song, it produces a series of chords. When it is used as a solo instrument it plays drone as well as the melody, like a bagpipe. Apart from the *khen* there is, in Laos, an instrument of equal importance; that is the bamboo cross flute *khlui(khuy)*, identical with the Vietnamese flute of the same name and the Cambodian *khloi*. It has seven fingerholes and a very pure tone.

The *taphon* is a double-membraned drum with cylindrical corpus, similar to the Cambodian drum *sampho* and the *tapone* of Thailand. It is beaten by both hands. The membranes are tuned with a paste of rice flour and palm ash. The drum *song na* has an even longer cylindrical corpus and is identical with the drum of the same name in Cambodia and Thailand. Only one membrane is tuned with paste. The *khong* is called *gong vong* in Laos. The Vietnamese *gong vong lek* with penetrating sound, is known in Laos under the name *kong noi*. The deep-pitched Vietnamese *gong vong vai* is identical with the *khong nhai* of Laos. The small cymbals *sing* are used both in Laos as well as in Cambodia (where they are called *tching*) to set the rhythm for the dancers and musicians.

THAILAND

The basis of instrumental music in Thailand is formed by the *piphat* orchestra made up of the shawm *pi nai* and percussion instruments. Percussion instruments are divided into melodious (xylophones, *gong* chimes) and rhythmic instruments (drums, metallophones of indefinite pitch). The leading instrument in the orchestra of Cambodia is the oboe *pey*, in Thailand its place is taken by a similar instrument, the oboe *pi nai*. It is slightly barrel-shaped with cylindrical bore and has six front fingerholes.

The mouthpiece consists of a short metal staple with double reeds of carefully selected dry palm leaves. This is taken in the mouth and blown in such a way as not to interrupt the air-stream during playing. The tone of the *pi nai* is penetrating and similar to that of the bagpipe. The lower tones are like grunts, the higher like squeals. In the *piphat* orchestra the *pi nai* usually accompanies the melody allotted to the *gong vong vai* embellishing it with variations.

The *ranad ek* is identical with the xylophone *ronéat-ek* of Cambodia. It is richly carved and inlaid with mother-of-pearl and ivory. The slabs are tuned by applying a heated mixture of bee's wax and lead filings to their front ends. In the *piphat* orchestra the *ranad ek* provides variations at the octave to the main melody usually played on the *gong vong vai*. The *gong vong lek* is somewhat smaller than the *gong vong vai*. It is tuned one octave higher and often doubles the main melody. The *ranad thume (thume mai)* is somewhat broader and slightly different in shape with seventeen deeply sounding slabs, hide-and-seek in the orchestra by doubling, retarding or dividing the melody with the help of large intervals. Further there are the metallophones *ranad thong ek (ranad lek)* with twenty-one steel slabs and the *ranad thong thume (thume lek)* with seventeen steel slabs which is deeper in sound.

The group of rhythmical instruments is mainly made up of membranophones. The *tapone* is a large barrel drum with the corpus hollowed-out of a single block of teak with heads of slightly different diameters. The right head, of ox or goatskin, is the larger; the left is of calfskin. Each is laced in zigzag pattern with leather thongs. Tuning paste of rice flour and palm ash is applied to the centre of the membranes to obtain a deeper sound. The thicker and heavier the paste, the smaller the vibration of the membranes and the deeper the sound. The somewhat smaller and longer drum *song na* is made in the same manner. During performance it is held on the player's lap. The largest Thailand drums are the *klong thad*, always used in pairs. They rest on boards and are propped up with the aid of two crossed sticks so that the lower head can vibrate freely. Loud tones are produced with two heavy bamboo sticks.

The *mong* is a gong of indefinite pitch suspended from a tripod. Five to seven such gongs of varying size, suspended from a wooden frame, are used for special sound effects in the *piphat* orchestra. The *charb lek* is a pair of small cymbals (*charb* = = cymbals, *lek* = small) and the *charb vai* is a pair of larger cymbals of identical shape. Heavy-sounding cymbals *ching*, saucer-shaped and threaded by a cord, are identical to the Chinese cymbals *peng-sing*.

BURMA Before the birth of Christ several empires had been established on the present territory of Burma, which were under Indian influence. Burmese culture began in the thirteenth century (Pugam). The expression of the arts, including music, served, above all, the ruling classes especially in the sixteenth century, the era of the Taungu. Burma had close contacts with India from the very beginning of its development, and even though it was part of India from the nineteenth century up to its liberation after the Second World War, it cannot be said that Burmese music bears noticeable traces of these contacts. Nor was there any particular Chinese influence, though apart from the seven-tone series the five-tone series, called the Chinese scale, is used in Burma. Melodies based on the pentatonic scale are indeed an exception in Burmese music. Large orchestras play only during ceremonies and processions. For less important celebrations smaller orchestras are used comprising the bamboo cross flute *pillui (pilweh)*, the oboe *hne*, the bamboo clappers *waleko (valet kyong)*, the cymbals *pekkivo* or *ye-gwin* and the drums *sege*, *ozi* and *si*.

The set of drums *patwaing (sein)* is the king of Burmese instruments. It looks like a huge tooth-edged crown, more than one metre high, glistening with gold and semi-precious stones. The player sits on a little bench within the circle formed by the beautifully carved wooden frame and indicates the rhythm by beating the set of up to twenty-one drums, arranged according to size and suspended from the inner side of the frame, with his fingers. The gong chime *tjivuaing* arranged in a circle similar to the *patwaing* stands next to it. Again the player sits on a low stool in the middle of the circle and beats the twelve to eighteen small gongs tuned to extend over two octaves. The gong with bells *mangvuaing* and the xylophone *patala*, first known in

Burma in the fifteenth century, with nineteen bamboo slabs tuned a²—e⁵ must also be numbered among the idiophones.

Apart from the above-mentioned instruments the *auyen* orchestra includes the following strings: the bow harp *saung (tsaung)* with thirteen silk strings tautened with the help of cotton cords, whose shape recalls a swimming fish with tail raised, the *megyaun*, an instrument with three strings in the shape of a crocodile, the bowed *thro* identical with the instrument of the same name from Cambodia, and the bowed *rebab*, which is found throughout Asia. The *turr (duri)* with four strings is similar to the Indian *sarod*. Its Indian origin is confirmed by the fact that it possesses nine drone strings.

Burmese instrumental ensemble after E. J. Colstone

A liking for bronze drums by the countries of South-East Asia is obvious from the history of their music. These include the drum *ngok-ly* used until recently by the mountain inhabitants of Vietnam. Old written and pictorial records mention a large number of musical instruments, clearly influenced by their Chinese counterparts. In the fifteenth century, under the Le dynasty, an amazingly well-organized musical life existed in Vietnam, including an orchestra made up exclusively of wind instruments and drums. There were large religious and secular orchestras in the sixteenth and seventeenth centuries.

VIETNAM

A few bars of a popular Vietnamese melody for the violin *nhi*

Just as the speciality of Burma is the *patwaing*, so that of Vietnam is the *dan bau (dan bao, cai dan bao)*. This monochord is not known in any other country. The *dan bau* is unique in the simplicity and ingenuity of its construction. A string is fixed over a rectangular resonator 100 cm long and 10—12 cm wide. The string is fixed to a peg on the right end of the corpus and on the left it terminates in a gourd or wooden funnel, suspended from an elastic bamboo lever. By means of this lever the player stretches and loosens the string to produce tones of varying pitch on which the melody is built by placing the palm of the hand on the string, and plucking the string with a wooden stick held in the same hand. Lately the music of the *dan bau* has been increased in volume by electrical means. Sometimes the player puts a tin on the soundboard near the bridge to attain a more expressive tone. At other times the player shortens the string with two vertical bamboo wands thus dividing it into three unequal parts. This produces stronger basic tones at the expense of the harmonic tonal range. The *dan bau* may also be played with a bow and various sound effects resembling human voices can be produced with the help of the lever.

Vietnamese boy with monochord *dan bau*

The *dan day* with a long neck and high frets is identical to the *chapei* of Cambodia. The four strings are tuned to the fifth and plucked with the fingertips or a plectrum. The *dan day* was once used as the instrument accompanying women reciting poetry. Today it has a much wider range of use in North Vietnam in the sphere of concert music. It is therefore not really a folk instrument; neither is the lute *dan ty ba (cai dan ti)*, which in construction and appearance corresponds to the Chinese lute *p'ip'a*. The guitar *dan-nguyet* with two pairs of strings tuned to the fifth g—d¹ is of Chinese origin. The zither *dan thap luk* whose corpus is made from teak is regarded as a very ancient instrument in Vietnam. Teak is the wood used most frequently in the production of musical instruments in the Far East. The sixteen brass strings of the *dan thap luk* pass across the bridge to the tuning pegs. If the strings between tailpiece and bridge are tuned to G, A, c, d, e, g, a, b, c¹, d¹, e¹, g¹, a¹, c², d², e², then the other part of the strings which is also used in playing is tuned to c, A, B, F sharp, G, B flat, A, B, C, B, B flat, G sharp, A, c, B, B flat. The player plucks the strings with the fingers of the right hand using a plectrum and by pressing the strings between bridge and pegs with the left hand he produces the vibrato.

Wind instruments came to Vietnam from China, and some of them still have their Chinese names. The bamboo cross flute *sao*, (called *ong sao* in North Vietnam), is identical with the Chinese flute *ti*. The *ong sao* has six oval fingerholes and one which is closed by a thin strip of paper. Two others are used to suspend the instrument. The end-blown flute *ong tien* is somewhat longer than the *ong sao*. It is similar to the Mongolian *limba* and takes the place of cross flutes in smaller orchestras. All types of flutes, with very rare exceptions, are tuned to C and the entire diatonic scale can be played on them. The shawm *ken gia nam (cai ken)* recalls its Chinese and Korean counterparts not only by its conical bore, the pipe terminating in a brass bell, but also in sound. It is always accompanied by percussion instruments, in South Vietnam by the drum *bong*, the small kettle-drum *dan* and the cymbals *chap bat*. The double clarinet *ken doi* together with the *ken gia nam* form an inseparable pair during funeral ceremonies in North Vietnam. The *ken doi* has two short bamboo pipes, each of them with seven fingerholes. Between the first and second fingerhole, on the back of both pipes, there is a small hole serving to suspend the instrument from brightly coloured cords.

The *khen be, khen tai* or *khen meo* of Vietnam corresponds to the mouth-organ of Laos. In some regions the Jew's harp *dan moi* with cane reed is to be found. The tubular xylophone *dan to rung* recalling the Javanese *angklung*, is widespread in North Vietnam. The metalfounders of Hanoi supply the entire Far East with gongs which, in Vietnam, are used to make up an orchestra recalling the famous Russian horn music. Every player holds one gong in his hand and beats it with a soft mallet when it is his turn according to the melody. The orchestra consists of from seven to fourteen players. The instruments and repertoire are passed from generation to generation.

INDONESIAN ARCHIPELAGO

The Mongolian-Malayan world from Korea to the Sunda Islands is very rich and colourful from the point of view of music. Each of the many islands has its characteristic musical features, and each musical instrument its own name. Music has developed on these islands since the arrival of the first immigrants in the second millenium BC, but it has followed different roads. In the first few centuries AD, Indian-ruled states were formed in South-East Asia, on Java and Sumatra. They included the Empire of Sumatra which, during the eighth century, stretched as far as western and central Java. After a shift in power relations at the beginning of the ninth century further to the east, India rapidly lost its influence and was replaced by the Far East. From the fifteenth century onwards there are permanent traces of the influence of Arabic music, and from the sixteenth century European music also made itself felt.

TONAL SYSTEM

The basis of melody structure in Indonesia is the *patet*, which represents a general tonal system determining the hierarchy and functional interconnection of the separate tones within the chosen tonal series. A total of six such systems exist, half of them ruled by the *salendro* and the other half by the *pelog*. These tone series have been accepted by classic Indonesian music, and in theory they differ from one another mainly in that the *salendro* divides the octave into five equal intervals of about one and a quarter tones, whereas the *pelog* has seven tones of various sizes. In practice, though, two tones are omitted so that the *pelog* actually consists of five tones: two large thirds, one whole tone and two semi-tones. In Laos and Burma another way of tuning is used instead of the two above-mentioned: the whole octave is divided into seven equal intervals, each of which is somewhat smaller than a whole European tone. Each of the two tonal series has about three hundred scales. Many researches insist that there is a connection between the Javanese scales and the old Chinese pentatonic series, while others refute this idea.

GAMELAN

In Indonesia the European will be enchanted by the 'magic' of their music. It is used to accompany the movements of the graceful dancers in the fantastic shadow plays; it resounds again and again in Krung-Thep or on Bali, a constant wave of chords calling forth in the listener the image of the singing trees of the Arabian Nights. This is the music of the famous *gamelan* orchestras by whose charm anybody at all sensitive to Oriental music is overcome. The best *gamelans* of the past belonged to the native rulers. On Java the greatest native ruler had twenty-nine *gamelans*, the sultan eighteen. On Bali today there are so many that there is one *gamelan* per 250 inhabitants. They are guarded like valuable property and given poetic names such as the 'Solacing', 'Rain of Scents', 'Eternal as the Sea', and so on. There are three *gamelans* on Java whose place of activity as well as the instruments they include are strictly determined. On Bali there is a *gamelan* made up of metallophones. If *salendro* and *pelog* compositions are on the programme, then the *gamelan* must have at its disposal two groups of instruments with fixed tuning. In a *gamelan* consisting of from fourteen to seventeen instruments and one singer, there are certain groups of instruments with strictly determined functions.

The basic theme is controlled by the metallophones or *sarons*, which have developed from the xylophones over a period of more than a thousand years. Six slightly arched bronze slabs in *salendro* and seven in *pelog* are set above a wooden resonator, frequently carved to resemble a dragon. Since it does not exceed the range of one octave and since the basic melody is usually of a wider range, it is allotted to various kinds of *sarons*. The highest tones are produced by the *saron panerus* or *peking*, and the deepest by the *saron barung*.

Variations on the main theme are played on the gong chime *bonnang (bonang)*, which consists of a number of bossed gongs placed open-side down on a low wooden frame, and rested on taut strings. Fourteen are in *pelog* and ten in *salendro*. The end-blown flute *suling* and the unfretted spike fiddle *rebab* of Persian-Arabic origin, with its heart-shaped corpus and its neck merging with the body, play independently in contrast to the basic melody. Both instruments give the *gamelan* a heterophonous character. The main tones are strengthened by the *slentem gantung* or *gender panembung*, bronze slabs with the compass of one octave that are suspended above tube resonators. The large gong, *gong gede*, is struck to indicate the end of the main periods of the composition, and the metallophone *gong kemondong (gong kemodong)* marks the end of the separate movements. The latter gong consists of two large bronze bars suspended on crossed cords over a wooden resonator. The player simultaneously plays a small, dull-sounding, bronze kettle gong, called a *ketuk*.

The gong is one of the most important musical instruments of South-East Asia. It is first mentioned in a Chinese source dating from the sixth century. In the fol-

Indonesian musician playing the gong chime *bonang*

lowing centuries it was already currently used throughout the entire Malay Archipelago. It is not only popular because of its charming sound, but also because of the belief in its magic power. Gongs avert natural catastrophies, heal diseases and affect most human activities. From the point of view of music clearly sounding gongs are most valued. *Rejongs* from Java and Bali are two gongs differently tuned and nailed at both ends to a piece of wood. The player holds two *rejongs* of differing size on his lap and beats them with a mallet in contrasting rhythm. Indonesian instrument makers have perfected the art of gong making. Their work is centred in the workshops and foundries of the town of Samarang, Java. Their instruments are carefully tuned, the metallophones by filing, the xylophones by milling the slabs or by affixing wax to their underside.

The sound of the gongs is varied by the gentle tones of the metallophones *gender barung* and *gender panerus*, thin bronze bars suspended on cords in a carved wooden

Indonesian gong *ketuk* and *gong kemondong*

frame, usually above tubular resonators tuned in unison with their corresponding bars. In fast passages they are beaten with the left hand while the right hand beats other bars. Particularly charming variations are added by the *gender panerus*, which has a beautiful, high-pitched ring. The trough xylophone *gambang kayu* with its hollow sound forms a suitable contrast to the clearly-sounding bronze instruments. It consists of sixteen to twenty slightly curved wooden bars placed on a rectangular wooden resonator in the shape of a trough or cradle. The *gambang kayu* has a considerable compass of from 3½ to 4 octaves. Xylophones of a similarly high level of perfection were already depicted on the reliefs of the fourteenth-century Javanese temple Panataron and provide important information about the method of playing. When performing, the player holds a pair of mallets in both hands, always inclined towards one another at the same angle. This is identical to the way in which African xylophones are played: this is no mere matter of chance, for a certain connection between South-East Asia and the African continent via the Indian Ocean and the Zambezi Valley is confirmed also by a certain agreement in tuning.

The masterly performance of the *gamelan* to this day attracts a large audience and is gaining in popularity beyond the frontiers of Indonesia. Though the tonal series of the *salendro* and the *pelog* at the moment constitute a considerable obstacle between European and the traditional Indonesian manner of tuning, many western composers, beginning with Debussy and finishing with Messiaen, regard the music of the *gamelan* as a treasure trove of melodic fantasy, capable of enriching the quality of contemporary symphonism.

An interesting folk instrument that has come to the fore in Indonesia is the *angklung*. It consists of several bamboo tubes tuned in unison, octave or chords, and suspended within a closed frame. When the frame is shaken to and fro the tubes produce a hollow, somewhat dull sound, similar to that of cow bells. A number of *angklungs* may possess a compass of up to two octaves and can be used to play various melodies. The music of the *angklung* used to be underestimated but has become so popular nowadays that it is broadcast fairly regularly on the Indonesian radio.

Indonesian gongs: *suwukan*, three *kempul* and two *kenong*

In the north-western part of the archipelao, espgecially in Sumatra and Borneo, musical tradition has, since the first millennium AD, been influenced by Arabic-Muslim culture, which penetrated further to New Guinea and Celebes. The music of these islands differs in both character and instruments from the music of South-East Asia. The *gamelan* orchestra is no longer to be found, but only chamber orchestra combinations of such instruments as flute and *rebab*, zither and drum, mostly resulting in one-voiced strongly chromatic melodies.

Apart from the original Indonesian instruments (the Jew's harp *genggon* and the drum *kendang*), instruments of foreign origin are also to be found in Sumatra. They include the bamboo whistle flute *bangsi (bansi)*, with six fingerholes at the front and one at the back; the shawm *serunai* (the Persian *surnai*); a flat double membrane drum *marwas;* the tambourine *rebana* and possibly also the lute *gambus* with a piriform corpus of one piece. The *gambus* is to be found from Sumatra to Halmahera and from Borneo to Java. It is also evenly spread along the coast among the Arab population.

The two-tone bamboo 'tuning fork' *druri-dana*, which reached Indonesia from south China via the Philippines, is typical of the population of Nias. On Celebes it is called *rere*. Here the resonator is not formed by the player's mouth as is usual for Jew's harps, but by the lower pipelike part of the instrument, two holes placed opposite each other and two protruding reeds. During a performance the instrument is held in the right hand and struck with the left wrist. By stopping the holes the pitch of the *rere* may be lowered or raised by a third. On Nias it is the custom to play simultaneously on two instruments of differing size, the smaller of which produces a sound that is about one tone higher. If the larger instrument produces g, b, the other produces a, c sharp, i.e. a total of four tones forming the basis of most of the song of south Nias. An equally amazing instrument on south Sumatra is the fish rattle *oro-oro*, held half above and half in the water. It produces a rattling, rustling sound, and is used by shark hunters as a decoy.

Borneo, the inhabitans of which are mostly of Malay or Asian origin, has the least colourful armoury of instruments among all the large Indonesian islands. Only the Dayak living inland use original wooden rattles and other primitive instruments, such as their harp, which is similar to the African harp. The *angklung* reached Borneo from Java and the mouth-organ *kledi* came from China. On Java it has six or seven pipes. The *dragong* gongs used in Sarawak and attracting attention by their interesting shape come from China. The bamboo chime *senajong* comes from South-East Asia. It consists of a number of bamboo sticks struck with a small mallet.

Two string instruments used to accompany epic songs are typical of Celebes. The plucked *katjapi* has the shape of a slender boat and is richly carved. The bowed *keso-keso* (of the inhabitants of Makassar) or the *gesong-gesong* (of the Buginese) has a coconut shell as resonator, a long neck and one or two strings. It is often beautifully carved and coloured red, white and black. Other interesting instruments include: the rattle *tjuriga*, in the shape of a knife with rattling chains, and the *sinto*, consisting of two kinds of *lontar* leaves sewn up in cotton, folded over and tied together with a flat knot. The player gets hold of the knots, brings them together and then quickly pulls them apart so that the strips touch each other with characteristic noise. Various kinds of flutes, including nose-flutes, are decorated by decorations being burnt into them. A strangely shaped drum is to be found on the island of Tanimbar. It has slits, is exposed to the wind and serves as a scarecrow. The orchestras, constantly increasing in number, not only try to preserve but also to develop further those aspects of ancient traditions possessing enough durability. Only the future will show what elements from European culture are recognized and accepted by Indonesian music. As history has shown, the musical genius of this country has always been able not only to absorb organically different external stimuli, but often also to raise them to a high artistic level.

AUSTRALIA AND OCEANIA

Tree gong of the Maori

Geographically Australia and Oceania comprise the territory of the aborigines of Australia and the islands of the Pacific: Melanesia, Micronesia, Tasmania, Papua and Polynesia. These geographical terms, however, do not coincide with the boundaries of musical culture, many of which are still largely unexplored. For centuries Oceania has been influenced to a greater or smaller extent by the differing cultures and musical traditions of the immigrants. This applies in particular to the music of Melanesia, which contains all forms of musical expression from the most primitive to the most highly developed.

The music of the Australian aborigines is above all vocal. Every Australian tribe has its own bard, keeping alive traditions both sacred and profane. On the islands of Oceania, music has a polyphonic character. In the Solomon Islands part-song excels above the play of pan-pipes, which in itself is polyphonic. Thanks to missionaries, songs that on Hawaii produced the so-called Hawaiian style are widespread, as well as the Hawaiian guitar that came to Hawaii from Europe. Hardly anything has been preserved of the original music of the Maori in New Zealand. Contemporary Maori melodies have been mainly taken from the European settlers, and above all from the missionaires. The Maoris, who possess a good ear for music and a natural feeling for harmony, quickly assimilated the style and spirit of the religious hymns and gave up almost completely their previous monotonous psalms.

The simplest forms of music are represented by a considerable number of sound instruments especially in such cultures where sounds are regarded as the spirits' voices. The Australians use a pair boomerangs, the Canacua sticks or pieces of bark, and the Maoris thump the ground with bamboo sticks. Apart from primitive bull-roarers such as the *pulai* in Hawaii, the *tetere* used by the Maori, and the singing splinter *niau kani* in New Zealand these instruments include vessel rattles (gourd and wood) in Hawaii, the *uliuli* etc. The *didjeridu* is most typical for Australia. It is made of bamboo stumps or hollowed-out wood into which the player blows at regular intervals, at the same time continuously muttering the word 'didjeridoo, didjeridoo...' An important autochthonous instrument in Hawaii is the *ipu*, a stamping vessel. It consists of a large calabash with a smaller one attached; apart from being stamped against the ground it is also beaten with the fingers. Signalling instruments of the Maori include the slit drum *pahu* suspended from a frame on a raised platform, and also the tree-gong, carved out of a tree trunk.

Many instruments are used for other purposes than that of simply making primitive music. Apart from the slit drum *pahu* the mortar drums *ihara* and *puniu* are used in Tahiti to pass on news, and in Hawaii the marine-shell trumpet *pu* and in New Zealand the *putatara* serve the same purpose. In the Greater Hebrides the setting up of large cylindrical drums with shark-skin membranes marks the beginning of ceremonies accompanied by song. The two heads of these drums are beaten alternately when relaying news and instructions. The slit drums to be found throughout the Pacific are often carved in human form, to represent ancestors that speak when the drums are struck. Bull-roarers are carved before the birth of a child and hidden in a cave. When the child is born the bull-roarer is placed in its cradle as the embodiment of the child's ancestor. Among the Semangi tree trunks lying on the ground are struck with sticks. The *pakuru*, as they are called in New Zealand, are concussion sticks that in Australia and the Pacific region originated from the belief in rain magic, in which two sticks represent lightning and cloud.

(♩ = 110)

Melody for nose flute according to Andersen

Apart from panpipes made up of eight reeds, there are also globular flutes made of gourds (called *hokiokio* and *pua* in Hawaii and New Zealand), notched flutes (called *koauau*, *poretu*, *whio*, and *rehu* in New Zealand) and nose-flutes (in Hawaii called *ohe-ohe-hano-ihu*, *fangofango*, and on Tahiti *vivo*). Jew's harps made of bamboo are called *niau kani* in Hawaii and *roria* in New Zealand. Chordophones are limited for all practical purposes to the musical bow *ukeke* in Hawaii which is used for speaking to the ghosts. Reed zithers have been found only in Melanesia.

The small guitar *ukelele* was brought to Hawaii by Portuguese workers. There it became the favourite instrument of an officer who was nicknamed 'Ukelele' (jumping flea, because he was small), and this nickname has become the name of the instrument.

Malay nose flute *semai-senoi*

41. Female mythical figures playing on lute, flute, drums and bells

42

42. Indian princess with *vina*

43

43. Famous officials from Akbar's court

44

45

44. Indian musician playing the *surbahar*

45. Indian bowed chordophone *mayuri* or *tagus* (peacock)

46. South Indian *vina*

47. North Indian *vina*

48

48. Statuette of a woman playing a stringed instrument

49

50

49. Bengal drum *dugdugi*

50. Copper horn *ranasringa*

51. Bengal drum *dhola*

52

52. Indian woman with *tambura*

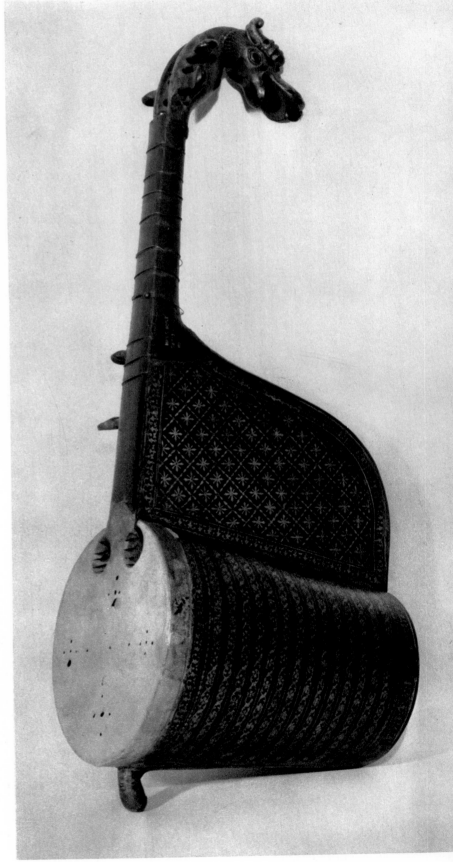

53. Indian *rebab*

54. Indian *sringara*

55. *Sarinda* from Bengal

56. *Sarinda* from Baluchistan

57

58

59

60

57. Indian drum *pillagovi* and monochord *pena*

58. Indian singer with *sarangi*

59. Indian *sarangi*

60. Musicians from Madras

61. Performance on the shawm *shanai*
62. Performance on the *mohori*
63. Indian horn *ranasringa* with double bell

62

63

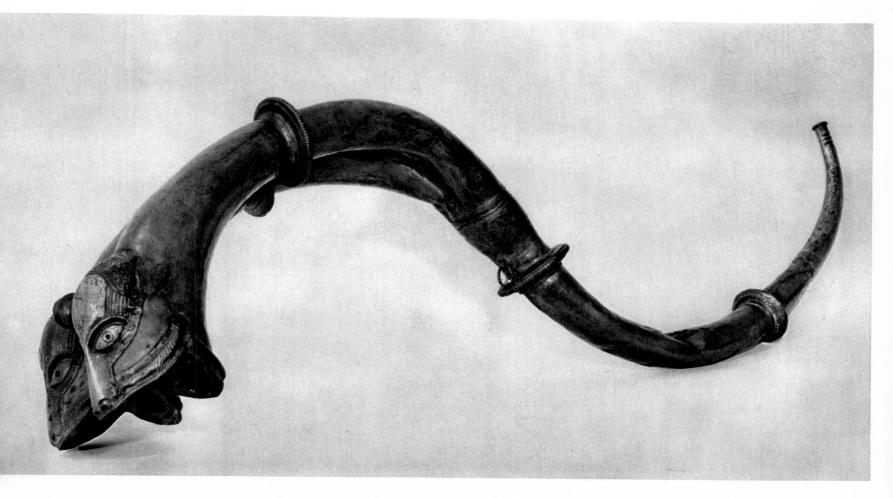

64

65

66

64. Indian drums *baya* and *tabla*

65. Indian musician playing the small drum *damaru*

66. Indian boys with drums *dapla*

67. Indian with drum *tudum*

68. Indian musician with *mandi*

67

68

69. Indian dance accompanied by drum *dhola*

70. Bass-relief from the temple at Angkor Wat

71

72

71. Cambodian guitar *chapei*

72. Instrumental ensemble of magi from Cambodia

73. Shawm *sralay* and horn *shaing* (*plom*)

74. Musicians of the court ensemble of Cambodia

75

75. Cambodian monochord *sa din*

76. Cambodian instrument *takhe* (crocodile)

77. *Tro-u* or *so-u* of Cambodia

78. Cambodian xylophone *ronéat-ek*

76

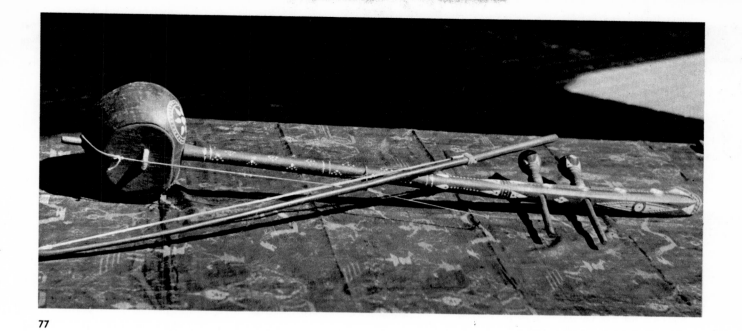

77

78

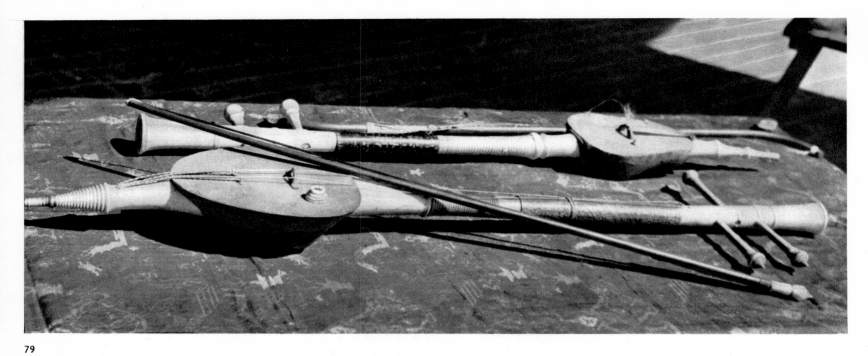

79

80

81

82

79. Cambodian spike fiddles
tro-khmer

80. Cambodian drums *skor*
and *romanea*

81. Cambodian drum
skor-thom

82. Drum *taphon* from Laos

83

83. Musician from Laos playing the mouth-organ *khen*

84.—85. Royal mohori ensemble in Luang Prabhang

84

85

86. Instruments of the Javanese gamelan

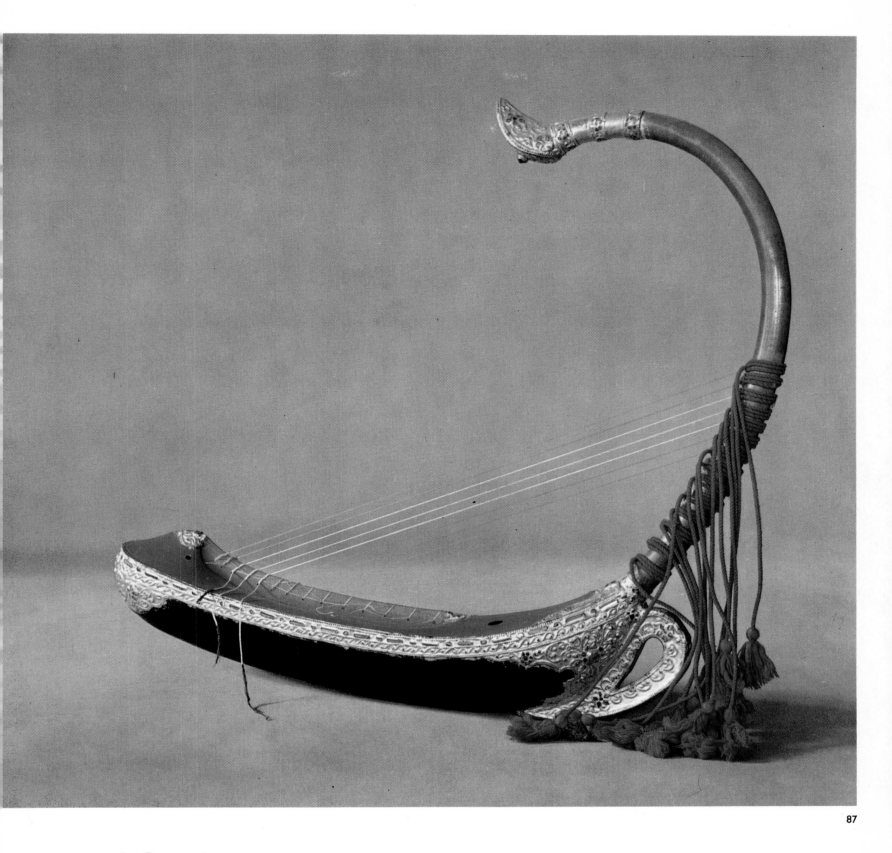

87. Burmese harp *saung*

88

88. Cambodian ensemble at Pi Phat

89. Lute *gambus* of the Dayaks from Borneo

90

91

90.—91. Musicians playing gong-chimes from Borneo

92. Harp of the Dayaks

93. Dayak drummer

92

93

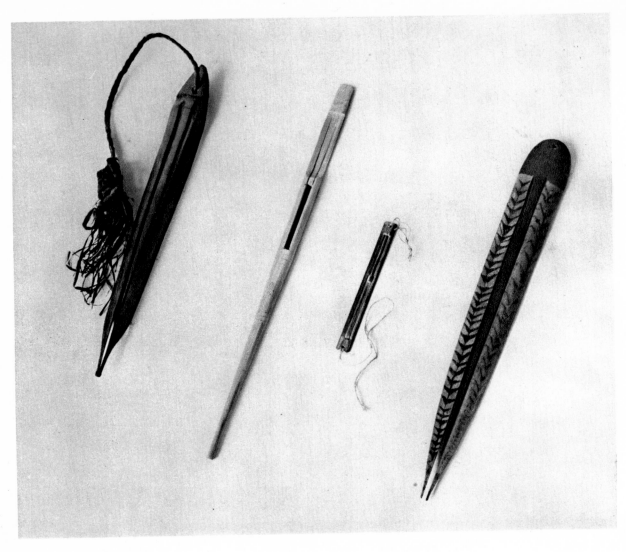

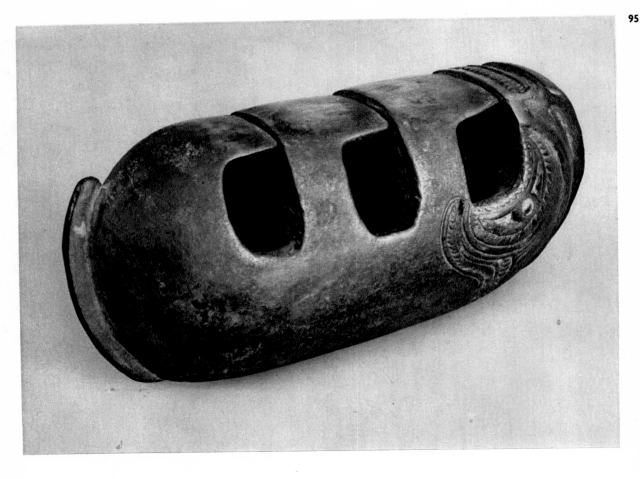

94. Jew's harp from Borneo and New Guinea

95. Friction xylophone *kulepa ganeg* (*nunut*) from New Ireland

96. One-headed drums from Oceania

97

97. Argentinian playing reed horn and drum

AMERICA

The musical culture of the Latin American peoples is the result of complicated reciprocal influences and the intermingling of European, American and African elements. Only very recently did scientists discover something about the music of the original inhabitants of the American continent, the American Indians, and archaeological finds have helped to throw at least some light on the hidden past of their music culture. It has been found that this was above all ritual, naturalistic, monotonous music. In the states where today the Indians are in the minority (Mexico, Brazil, Argentina) the colonizers succeeded in replacing this music by that of their own countries so thoroughly that the present folk music of Latin America has hardly any Indian musical elements. Two features prevail in Mexico, Central and South America: the European (Spanish and Portuguese) and the African (Negro). Only later did the influence of other nations make itself also felt (Italian, German). Where the population is made up mainly of Indians (Central America, Peru, Bolivia, etc.) the influence of Indian music is much stronger. Original Indian music has become very rare and exists only in some tribes of Mexico, Peru, Brazil, Argentina and Chile.

Indian melody recorded by Jean de Lery in Brazil in 1553

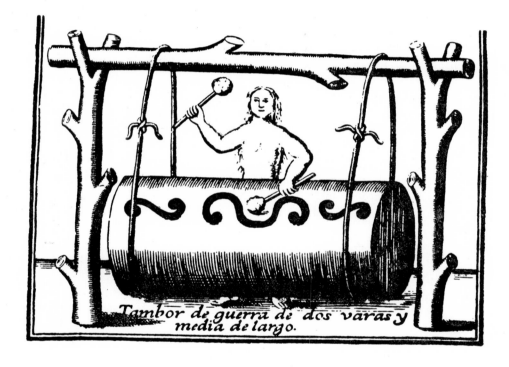

Indian slit drum of Venezuela. Woodcut after J. Gumilla, 1745

MEXICO

In the sixteenth century the Spanish missionary Juan de Torquemada described a Mexican Indian dance. This valuable eye-witness report on the performance of Indian music proves, together with pictures in old Indian manuscripts, that dancing, singing and instrumental music were regarded as one. Music was considered to be an important expression of life, a gift of the gods and an essential feature in all ceremonies. The Indians even had their god of music called Macuilxochitl or Xochipilli

'. . . When the dancers arrive at the place, they take their place to play the instruments. The two best singers then begin the song. A large drum, played with the hands, is called a huehuetl. The other, played with sticks like the instruments of Spain, is called the teponaxtli . . . Wishing to begin the dance, three or four Indians raise very shrill whistles. The instruments sound in a low tone, and little by little increase in volume. When the dancers hear the instruments they begin to sing and dance. The first song goes slowly and in a deep tone. When one song is finished, the instrument changes tone, and the leaders begin another chant, a little higher and more lively. In this way, the songs keep rising, as though someone changed from a bass to a tenor voice.'

Juan de Torquemada

Aztec musicians with rattles *ayacaztli*, drums *teponaxtli* and *huehuetl*. After a miniature from the Aztec Codex

Song of the Maya warriors after B. Foster

Mexican dancer with rattles *sonaja* and *tenabaris* and jingles *cascabelles*

by the Aztecs. The slit drum *teponaxtli (teponaztli)*, with the corpus made in one piece, was played only on festive occasions. Often it was carved in the shape of an animal — an alligator, puma or ocelot. It had an opening in the bottom and an H-shaped slit in the top creating two tongues facing each other. The interior was chiselled away to leave different thicknesses of wood so that the tongues, when struck with two wooden beaters, produced tones of different pitch. The single-headed drum *huehuetl* was also made of one piece. Its Mayan name *zacatan* indicates the rhythm of the anapaest (UU —) expressed in music by two short notes and one long. This rhythmic figure, two sixteenths and one eighth (♫ ♪), occurs in the song of the Mayan warriors. The *huehuetl* was covered with jaguar or stag skin either laced with strings in the same way as a parchment membrane is fixed when fruit is bottled, or nailed. The *ayotl*, consisting of the carapace of a huge turtle, and depicted in wall paintings in Bonampak and in the Becker Codex, was a scraper and not a drum as some researchers think. The uneven surface was scraped with deer's antlers or a stick.

The five centuries that have passed since the day when the first European set foot on the soil of Mexico have changed the very foundations of the character of Mexican folk music. If we study Indian music with Creole features stretching from Ecuador to the northern part of Argentina, then in Mexico we meet exclusively Creole music with negligible Indian elements. Pure remnants of the music of the original inhabitants of Mexico may be found only in the most remote parts of the country. Apart from Creole music there is a very important cross-product, so-called mixed music, and in no other Latin American republic has it such an important position and such specific artistic importance as it has in Mexico. This is because the Spanish-Creole basic element prevails absolutely and the Indian element is only slightly represented, though it is of great importance artistically. Extraordinary smoothness, elements of prosody in strict Castillian metres, a tendency to chromatics, organically combined with the 'oriental' melodies of Andalusian origin — that is the contribution of the descendants of the Aztecs to contemporary Mexican musical culture.

A considerable number of Indian instruments are still being used in Mexican folk music. The scraper *raspadero (raspador, tzicahuaztli)*, a dentated gourd or notched wooden stick that is scraped with a bamboo stick, dates from the Stone Age. A huge scraper of whale bone has been discovered in Monte Albano, which has four sound registers produced by four rows of notches differing in width. The pellet jingle *sonaja (sonajas, ayacaztli)* — the dried fruit of the gourd filled with pebbles — corresponds with the *maraca* of Cuba and Brazil. *Cascabelles* are small rattles of beads, dried seed, clay or tin. The pellet bells *tenabaris*, made of dried butterfly cocoons which dancers tie to their ankles, are also one of the din-producing instruments. The *jicara de agua* is a kind of water drum consisting of a larger gourd submerged with its cut-off upper end in a water-filled vessel. The instrument is struck with a stick whilst another stick is used to 'tune' it by submerging it more or less into the water.

The *chililihtli (chilitli)*, a cross flute of terracotta, is used as the accompanying instrument for almost all native dances (in the region of Veracruz the God of Music Xochipilli used to be represented as a smiling figure in the shape of a flute). The *tlapitzalli* is a type of end-blown flute. The upper end is closed except for a very narrow duct into which the musician blows, and which directs the air-stream to the sharp edge of a lateral hole. The beaked mouthpiece enables the player to grip the instrument tightly with his lips. Three to five fingerholes are placed without regard to any metrical rules. The shawm *chirimia* is mentioned in ancient chronicles and played to this day in the state of Mexico and many parts of the Mexican republic. It is unusual in that the player inhales instead of exhaling, to produce a plaintive, sorrowful sound. The *chirimia* is played at midnight from the church towers, especially during Holy Week. The marine-shell trumpet *atecocolli*, to be found in pre-Colombian times along the entire coastline, produces only several booming tones that inspired the Mexican composer C. Chavez (1889) in his work named after the Aztec god of music Xochipilli. In his symphonic works Chavez also prescribes other native Indian instruments such as the drums *huehuetl* and *teponaxtli*.

The Indians' only string instrument seems to have been the musical bow *tahuitol* (the *mitote* of the Cora Indians) used in the north west of Mexico. Apart from the

Mexican pipe *fluviol* with tabor *tambori*,
water drum *jicara de agua* and scraper
raspadero

Mexican folk musicians

wooden bow it has a gourd resonator. The musician holds the instrument with the aid of a stick on which his right leg rests. The strings are struck with two thin sticks. The confirmation of the existence of this instrument among the Maidu Indians on the western slopes of the Sierra Nevada completely refutes the view that the musical bow was brought to America by the negroes. The basis of folk music, not only in Mexico but throughout Latin America from Patagonia to the Rio Grande, is the Spanish guitar. The harp was also brought to Latin America; unlike the European harp it is played standing up. The Indians from the state of Sonora use the mono-chord *eeneg* or *enne* to accompany dancing, and their long rectangular corpus recalls the European monochord, and square pegbox the Indian *sarangi*. It has neither fingerboard nor frets and the bridge is shifted to the lower part of the corpus. The clumsy bow has one string instead of horsehair.

CENTRAL AMERICA

Central America and the Caribbean area presents a hard nut to crack to the inquisitive ethnomusicologist, since the topographical conditions and utter dissimilarity in population prevents the formation of a uniform picture of musical folklore. This problem, however, is not unique in this region only and is met practically throughout Latin America. Here it is particularly marked, since some Indian tribes have a very low level of civilization, while others must be regarded as the descendants of peoples with a very high culture such as the Mayas and Aztecs. The whites, the descendants of the Spanish, are most uniform in cultural level, whereas the Negro population again shows considerable differences in their degree of civilization. And just as the population of Central America greatly differs, so does their distribution in the Central American and Caribbean area. The Indians are settled in the mountain regions and the jungles, the Negroes in the tropical coastal zone and on the islands, the whites in the towns and their close vicinity. Musical life is closely connected with this distribution of the population. In the town it is European; on the outskirts Negro music prevails and in the countryside remnants of Indian music have been preserved.

CUBA

The original Indian music on the largest Central American island, Cuba, was soon ousted by the influence of Negro music. The Negroes escaped from Haiti and the Dominican republic and settled in Cuba, where today Negroes and mulattoes form one-third of the population. They created one of the most important centres of Afro-American music in which instruments imported from Africa are mostly used. Idiophones and membranophones stressing rhythmical elements are most strongly represented. Wind and string instruments are fewer in number. The Cubans' particularly well developed feeling for rhythm enables them to turn practically anything into a musical instrument. And so baking tins, plates, spoons, even hoes without handles and ploughshares may be used. A favourite instrument throughout Central America is the *claves*, Cuban concussion sticks, consisting of two cylindrical hardwood sticks, made of grenadillo or guaiac wood. One stick is held in the cupped left hand and forms a kind of resonator when struck with the other stick. The sticks produce a

114

metallic sound whose pitch depends on the point at which one stick strikes the other. The *claves* and not the *maracas*, as is often wrongly stated, determine the firm rhythmic structure of the music by their distinct, unchangeable rhythm.

Metallophones consist of various bells such as the *ekon*, forged and welded to resemble the letter U and provided with a handle, that is struck with a metal stick. The *agogo* is a tulip-shaped bell with clapper, usually provided with a handle. The *enkanika* is a square clapper bell. The metallophones include the *marimbula*, which has nothing in common with the *marimba* but is identical with the African *sansa*. Rattles hold an important position among Afro-Cuban instruments. There are two main variants: the *guira* or *agbe* (also called *sapo*) and the *maracas*. The *guira* is made from the dried fruit of the *Lagenari vulgaris* which occurs everywhere in the Tropics. Filled with nuts or glass pellets, its surface is covered with a net of thin strings. The *guira* is played by holding it in the right hand by the small knot, closing the opening of the gourd and beating it with the left hand on the other side. The *maracas* is also made from the dried fruits of gourd trees and is filled with dry seed or pebbles. In Europe it is known as the 'rumba rattle'. A rattle that can also be used as scraper is the *kiyada*, a typically Afro-Cuban instrument. It consists of the dry jawbone of an ass, mule or horse, to which pellet bells are attached. When the instrument is shaken, the teeth loosely tied to the *alveoli* rattle, or a rattling sound may be produced when a stick is scraped along the teeth.

The number of drums playing a most important part in Afro-Cuban music is boundless. This is proved by the fact that in Cuba there exist orchestras made up entirely of drums. The *joca (yuka)* is used to accompany folk dances. It is a cylindrical, single-headed drum of Congolese origin. The membrane of ox or calf skin is first nailed down and then slightly moistened and heated over the fire to stretch it further. The *joca* exists in three sizes: the *caja* is the largest and always in the centre of the orchestra; on its right is the *mula* and on its left the small *cacimba*. The instrument is played in the same way as it is to this day in Africa, i.e. it is gripped by the musician's knees who sits on it as if it were a saddle. This also explains the general name of the drums —'tambor montado' — riding drum. It is beaten with fingers and palms, and sometimes with mallets. The *conga*, a barrel drum with one head, made of boards and strengthened with metal hoops, is a great favourite in Afro-Cuban orchestras. The *bongo* consists of two conical drums slightly different in size, joined together horizontally, and gripped between the musician's knees. A high degree of skill may be attained both on the *bongos* as well as on the *conga* by a special technique of fingers and palms in which not even *glissando* is lacking.

No wind instruments are used in Cuban folk music apart from the primitive globular flute *botija*. This is an earthenware jug with a narrow neck and lateral opening used as a mouthpiece. The pitch of the tone is changed to a certain extent by the musician's right hand on the neck of the vessel. The *lauto de garrocio*, a stick flute, is widespread among the young people. It is made from a cutting of a hollow branch or bamboo. One end of the tube is open, the other covered by a thin plant membrane. Near the membrane is an opening into which the musician sings. The membrane increases the volume of the human voice and turns it into nasal sounds.

Some primitive instruments are used by Negro musicians in the eastern part of Cuba, including the musical bow with gourd resonator called *sambi* and the ground harp *tumbandera* (also called *tingotalango* or *kimbumba*.) The construction of this 'harp' is very interesting. Next to the flexible trunk of a young tree a pit is dug and covered with a resonance board with a small opening in the centre. Through this a string with a knot is passed and tied to the bent-over tree top. Then tree is released so that the string is extended to the full. The musician plucks the string and if he is skilful he can even produce some flageolet tones by lightly touching the knotted points of the string. The guitar *tres* with three drone strings is the most widely used European string instrument. The *tipplo (tiple)* was originally a soprano variation of the guitar, but later became a modification of the *pandura* with three or four drone strings. Its present shape recalls a flat mandolin. The banjo is naturally a great favourite, and is also used as a drum. The strings are removed and the leather-covered lid struck with the fingers.

Cuban player with rattle *maracas*

HAITI

When the first explorers came to Haiti, it was the legendary Queen Anacaona herself who danced a native dance for them. In the present music of the island there are no traces at all of the music of the original population. It is entirely under the influence of Negro music. Music in Haiti means the sound of the drums that accompany the Haitians from their childhood onwards and is to be heard at every private or public event. In character the Haitian drum music is polyrhythmical. Small drums have a fast and mobile rhythm, large drums stress the heavy beats. The Haitian drums are named after the members of the family. The largest drum whose sound, so the people believe, affects even the dead is called *mamma drum*. Then there is a *father drum* and a *baby drum*. There is also a working drum — the *tambour travaille* and the *assotor*, which is supposed to be sensitive enough to react to the slightest wind, like an Aeolian harp. Due to its close relation to the drums, the people of Haiti also call the ground harp a drum. The *maracas* in Haiti bear the onomatopoeic name *chacha*. The primitive bamboo pipe *vaccine* is one of the native wind instruments. There exist a large number of percussion instruments made of various materials depending on the occasion.

DOMINICAN REPUBLIC

Folk instruments in the Dominican Republic include, apart from the all-powerful guitar which is here called *maricuba*, such native instruments as the scraper *guayo*, the gourd rattle *guajey*, the castanets *tuti* and the slit drum *maguey*. The marine-shell trumpet is called *cobo* and there is a horizontal drum with one head — *balsie tumbado*. The ground harp *gayumba* that must have been brought to San Domingo from Cuba consists of a flexible rod struck in the earth beside a pit covered with boards. The string fixed between the end of the rod and the lid of the pit is plucked with the fingers.

GUATEMALA

Guatemala is the home of the *marimba*, a xylophone with gourd resonator called *goyom* by the natives. Though the *marimba* comes from Africa, its name is found more often today in connection with Central America and especially Guatemala where it has been a folk instrument for centuries. The largest *marimba* has 137 chromatically tuned slabs with an eleven-octave compass and the same number of resonators. The resonators have a tiny opening at the end covered with a thin membrane of pig gut, serving to prolong the fading sound. The slabs of the *marimba* are arranged in two main registers. The upper 'marimba' register has a six-octave compass and the lower 'tenor' register has a five-octave compass. To make full use of the instrument seven well-trained musicians are required. A smaller number of musicians suffices for a smaller *marimba*. Other instruments in use in Guatemala are the slit drum called *tunzu* or *hul. Tsihali (tzijolay)* is a type of end-blown flute and the *tot* is a marine-shell trumpet.

HONDURAS AND SALVADOR

In Honduras and Salvador there is a marked Indian influence in music. A special kind of whistling statue, made of clay and representing a man sitting at a barrel with two interconnected hollows, has been discovered. If these hollows are filled with water and the barrel moved from side to side, the air is driven into the whistle heads and a whistling sound is produced. The slit drum *teponahuaste* and the *zambumbia* with string lacing are the most frequently used drums in Salvador. The *carimba* is a special kind of musical bow. A metal string is fixed to both ends of a wooden box in the manner of a monochord.

NICARAGUA

The same musical bow is called *quijongo* in Nicaragua, and is further fitted with a mobile bridge. A friction drum *juco* is also in use, consisting of a barrel covered with a membrane through which a string passes that must be rubbed with the palms. The primitive trumpet *cacho* is made of an animal horn. The *chilchil* is a small bell used by the natives. The *ieumai* is a rattle of the same type as the *maracas* and the *cubarro* is a kind of transverse flute.

COSTA RICA AND PANAMA

Among the archeological finds in Costa Rica and Panama the attention of musicologists has been attracted by some clay objects that might have been drums though they differ considerably from the Mexican types. Their plastic decoration, elongated cuts and belt indicate the use of string for stretching the head. Folk music in Costa Rica today is represented by the street song *callejeras* accompanied by a guitar called *mejoranera* in Panama, since it is used to accompany the dance *mejorena*. The *bocana* is a larger type of guitar. During the girls' initiation rites among the Cuna Indians a trial by ordeal is held. Two flutes made of pelican wings called *horki-kala* are wrapped up in the leaves of a tree. If the musician unwraps them and finds the flutes in the original position, the girl is a virgin; if they are lying the other way round, she is not. In Panama three types of drums exist differing from one another in size — the small *repicador*, the medium *pujador* and the large *tambor*. An artist on the *repicador* enjoys the same popularity as the best violinist or pianist in Europe.

Polyrhythmic scheme of the Dominican dance tune *merengue* after J. M. Cooper-Smith

SOUTH AMERICA

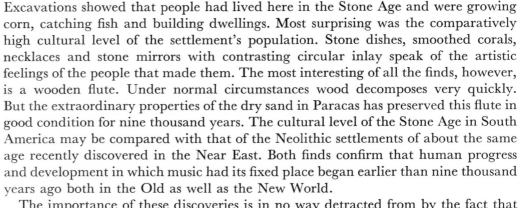

PERU

In 1964 a nine-thousand-old settlement was discovered near Paracas in Peru. Excavations showed that people had lived here in the Stone Age and were growing corn, catching fish and building dwellings. Most surprising was the comparatively high cultural level of the settlement's population. Stone dishes, smoothed corals, necklaces and stone mirrors with contrasting circular inlay speak of the artistic feelings of the people that made them. The most interesting of all the finds, however, is a wooden flute. Under normal circumstances wood decomposes very quickly. But the extraordinary properties of the dry sand in Paracas has preserved this flute in good condition for nine thousand years. The cultural level of the Stone Age in South America may be compared with that of the Neolithic settlements of about the same age recently discovered in the Near East. Both finds confirm that human progress and development in which music had its fixed place began earlier than nine thousand years ago both in the Old as well as the New World.

The importance of these discoveries is in no way detracted from by the fact that the cultural level in the period between the year 2000 and the eighth century BC, when the Aymara and Incas ruled Peru, was lower than in Central America. It is extraordinary that music here nevertheless attained a higher level of development, as is indicated by archeological finds and musical motifs on vases. Pan-pipes with many tubes and flutes with fingerholes speak of complicated melodies and also lead us to believe that cultures older than that of the Incas must have already known other scales than the pentatonic one. An explanation why the Incas did not take over the rich melodic material of such civilizations as that of the Nazca, Chima and Tiahuanaco may perhaps be found in the symbol of the hand with five fingers which was of special importance in the life of the Incas. The hand of the god Pachacamaco has been preserved on several gold and stone statues. Therefore it is the special system based on the number 5 and not any possible contact with the Far East that explains why the intervals between the fingerholes of the Peruvian flutes deviate only slightly from the oldest Chinese flutes.

Original Inca melody after A. Sas

More than ten thousand years have passed since the oldest flute ever discovered on the territory of Peru was completed, but it has remained the most typical instrument of the Peruvian Indians to this day. This is the flute *qena (kena)* made from bamboo or the bones of a llama leg. Originally it had five fingerholes, but under the influence of Spanish music it was adapted to the intonation of the diatonic scale. A flute of the same type though shorter is the *mala*. The *tede* is made of bird bones. The pan-pipe known throughout South America is called *antara* in Peru. Of the great variety of colourful globular flutes the one typical in Peru imitates various kinds of conches. The folk *ocarina* of today is called *ayariche*. The primitive tube made of wood or terracotta *aylliquepa* (also *hayllai-quipac* or *tock oro*), capable of producing only a few harmonic sounds, is the descendant of the short clay tubes that evidently belonged to the early period of Peruvian civilization. The Incas knew some idiophones, and rattles made from gourds, conches and nutshells. They also had pellet bells and strange square wooden bells similar to those still in use in Burma and the western part of the Malaysian peninsula. The *sukcha* is a percussion instrument made from a llama skull. The *maracas* is here called *chil-chil*. So far it has not been possible to verify whether the clear-sounding, round, slightly concave-convex metal plates found in ancient Peruvian tombs were indeed gongs.

Two types of drums prevail in Peruvian folk music: the barrel drum *tynia* with two heads and the *huancar* with one head that can be tuned. Human skin was once used for these drums. One king of the Incas had his treacherous chieftains skinned alive. The skins were blown up and then used as drums.

Bolivia, in the heart of South America, far from the sea-shore, is one of the four regions into which the Empire of the Incas once used to be divided. There hardly exists a more natural frontier in the world than that between Peru and Bolivia, formed by Titicaca, the holy lake of the Incas. The Bolivian banks are inhabited by the descendants of the Aymara Indians and some distance from the lake there live the Quechua Indians. They speak the same language as their brothers in Peru and Ecuador, they worship the sun and play the same type of instruments. The *pincullu* is identical with the *pingullo*, the endblown flute of Ecuador. The endblown flute *kena* with three to seven fingerholes is identical to the Peruvian *qena*. Similar flutes of different dimensions are the *charka* (also *charge, cankara*) and the *senka*. They are cut from halved and hollowed branches; then the two halves are fitted together again and tightly bound with fresh plant fibres. An interesting example of the migration

Indian musicians from Ecuador

of folk instruments over great distances is the bass flute *aykhori* which is similar to the Slovak *fujara* not only in structure but also in dimensions. It was probably imported to Bolivia by Slovak immigrants in the nineteenth century. But the typical instrument of the Bolivian armoury is the pan-pipe *sico (sicus)*. It consists of seven to seventeen pipes closed at the bottom and connected in one or two rows. The Aymara Indians have *sico* orchestras of six to forty instruments arranged in groups according to size. This is guided by the simple and unchangeable principle that the longest pipe of the smaller *sico* is exactly half as long as the larger *sico*. In the Lake Titicaca region the *sico* is made of pipes of the same length. The pipes are joined together top and bottom and tuned with sand poured into them. The *sico* is held upright so that the lower lip of the musician rests on the edge of the opening. However, he never lets the instrument glide quickly along his lips as the Rumanian pan-pipe players do, but blows every tube separately with a slight smacking of the tongue producing a staccato sound. The *bajon* looks like a huge pan-pipe. It is an instrument with the mouthpiece made from twisted bark strengthened with terracotta. The name of the war trumpet *pututu* is a synonym of the South American drums, consisting of a wooden cylinder with a bell made from the horn of a bull.

119

Lithophones and pan-pipes dating back to the pre-Colombian era have been found in Ecuador and exact copies are being made to this day by the natives from bamboo or condor feathers and called *rondador*. The flute *pingullo* is identical to the Peruvian end-blown flute *qena* and the *chil-chil* with the rattle *maracas*. The guitars *charango* and harps seem to have been brought here from Mexico.

COLOMBIA

The collections of the Museum of Fine Arts at Boston contain a gold statue made by the Quimbaya Indians in Colombia. It represents a musician playing a double nose-flute. Uitoto Indians dig a pit and cover it with boards. Then they place a big hollowed-out tree-trunk on four posts closely above the boards. When there is a full moon the women start to dance round the pit and the men stamp in the hollow tree-trunk which begins to swing, hitting the boards covering the pit and producing resounding tones. The slit-drum similar to the Mexican *teponaxtli* is called *manguara*. The *cununu* is a drum with one head. The *maracas* has spread here under different names such as *alfadoque*, *chucho*, *carangano*, etc. The Indians of Colombia know the musical bow — *timbirimba* — played by rubbing the string with a wooden stick.

VENEZUELA

In Venezuela lithophones similar to those of Ecuador have been found. J. A. Calcano described the secret rites of the natives in the jungle which are accompanied by the drums *botutos*. The drums *cumaco*, *curveta* and *mine* are of African origin and used by Negroes. The small drum *culo-en-tierra* (buttock in the earth) is rather an interesting instrument, consisting of half a coconut shell covered with a parchment membrane and placed in a small hole in the ground. The *juco* of Nicaragua is similar to the friction drum *furruco* producing a grunting sound when a string covered with resin and fixed to the bottom of the corpus is rubbed with the palms. The *dadoo* is a rattle of the *maracas* type and the *turá* is a cross-flute.

BRAZIL

The music of the largest country of the South American continent, Brazil, is a compound of the melancholic lyricism of Portuguese melodies, Negro rhythm and an admixture of Indian elements. The Portuguese conquerors and the African slaves brought their own musical tradition with them to Brazil which exerted a reciprocal influence, and after mingling blossomed forth into the bright flower of Brazilian folk music. Later on Spanish, Italian, French and last but not least American jazz elements were added. Influenced by this development of folk music, instruments developed that particularly stressed rhythm. In Brazil they are fittingly referred to as *ritmadores*, creators of rhythm. The rhythm of the Brazilian folk music is comparable to the beating of the heart.

The same instruments often have different names in different parts of Brazil and (vice versa) the same names often indicate two quite different instruments. If we further take into account the names of innumerable variants and improvisations existing in all groups of instruments, then the etymological chaos is complete. The huge family of rattles is represented here by the *maracas* called *chocalho*, a pebble-filled tin cone. In Pernambuco it is called *xere*, in Bahia *adja*. Another type of *maracas* filled with seeds called the 'Tears of the Holy Virgin' strung on a frame is called *afoxe* or *piano-de-cuia*, also *xaquéxaqué* or simply *caboca*. In voodoo rites Negroes use the *agogo*, a double bell made of iron. Each bell emits a different sound when struck with a metal stick. The armoury of instruments of the Brazilian Negroes does not greatly differ from that of the Haitian or Cuban Negroes except for some names. For example, membrane drums of various shape and size are called *batá*, *batá-coto* and *carimba*. The ritual drum is *babacue*, the small flute *afofie* and the musical bow *bansa*. The Cataquinaru Indians of Central Brazil place great emphasis on 'earth drums'. They dig a hole in the ground into which they fit the hollow trunk of a palm tree filled with rubber, powdered mica and bits of animal bones. This tree-trunk is then used as a resonator on which they stamp during their dances.

The national instrument of Brazil is the guitar *violao* of Portuguese origin with five or six gut strings. It is tuned differently according to the region and the type of music for which it is used. Different tunings are recommended for various songs and dances to permit chords necessary to create the distinct harmony. The usual tuning is a, d^1, g^1, b^1, e^2 or e, a, d^1, g^1, b^1. In the past, when folk musicians held competitions in improvization on the *violao*, the victor used to tie coloured ribbons, symbols of victory, to the pegs of his instrument. Sometimes the *violao* is called *pinho*, after the

Player with the Brazilian drum *atabequé*

wood it is made from. In the state of Sao Paolo two types of guitars are to be found. On the coast there is the *litoral violao*, almost the same size as a European guitar, and in the mountains the *violao de serra-acima* or *violao paulista*. The *violao* of the coast is larger and has eight strings, seven of equal length. The eighth is shorter, and is called *cantadeira* (the singing string) and is fixed on a protuberance between the neck and the resonator. The *violao paulista* is made in various sizes. The smallest is called *mochinho*, *macheto* or *machetinho*. In some states the *violao* has twelve to fourteen strings. The *cavaquinho*, an instrument similar to the guitar, is of Portuguese origin. Its four strings are tuned d, g, b, d, and it is played with the fingers or a bone plectrum. Miraculously the three-string bowed *rebec*, *rabeca* or *rebeca* from the European medieval armoury of instruments has been preserved in its original shape. Village musicians who play it make their own instruments.

Chilean folk music developed under the influence of Spanish music, and this is why here too the guitar is the most widely used instrument. Only one hundred thousand of the five million people are Araucano Indians, and they live too far away from the cultural centres to have any influence whatsoever on Chilean national music. The music of the Araucano Indians differs considerably from that of the other South American Indians. Apart from the pentatonic scale they use intervals smaller than half-tone intervals. Despite their primitiveness their musical instruments often show inventiveness and fantasy. The Araucano possess the longest bamboo trumpet, *trutruca*, more than two metres in length and producing only one tone. A small, primitive type of flute with three or four fingerholes is called *pifulka* and a tiny bamboo flute played by breathing strongly into it is known as the *lilkin*. A unique instrument from the point of view of construction is the double musical bow *kunkulkawe*. It consists of two wooden sticks or animal bones tied together with a string and inter-

South American guitar players

locked like a chain. It is played with a bow. Other instruments include : the rattle, *woda or huada* made of dried fruits filled with pebbles, the marine-shell castanets *cadacada*, the flat *cultrum* that is actually a drum, the end-blown flute *pinculwe* and the horn *culculwe (küllküll)*.

Indian music had negligible influence on the folk music of Argentina. Here, too, the guitar rules supreme in the hands of gaily dressed musicians accompanying pampas dances in extraordinarily fast tempi. Mountain dances, however, are accompanied by Indian instruments, the flutes *kena* and *aingullo*, the pan-pipe *sicura* and the small five-string guitar *charango*. In the north of the country the *hupjira*, made from a bull's horn, is played during festivities and celebrations. The Indians of Patagonia have a musical bow, *kohlo*, made from a horse's rib and horsehair, which is plucked by a condor feather. The sound produced is so weak that it is hardly audible more than two metres away.

121

In Paraguay and Uruguay more than one missionary was killed simply because the Guarani Indians wanted his bones to make their notched scraper *congorea*. Folk music in these states developed mainly under the influence of Creole music. *Memby* is the generic name for straight bamboo flutes used by the Indians in neighbouring Brazil. Various types of *memby* are named according to size: *memby-apara, memby-chue, memby-guazu, memby-tarara*. The *mure-mure, matapu* and *carugu* are drums. The native name for a *maraca*-like rattle is *mbaraca*. The *tore* is a primitive tube made of sugar cane or terracotta producing hoarse, plaintive sounds. In both states folk songs and dances are today accompanied by the guitar and accordion. The drum *tambouril* is a great favourite during carnivals and popular celebrations.

The process of the reciprocal influence of musical cultures in Latin America has not yet terminated. There exist synthetic forms that arose in the seventeenth and eighteenth centuries and also forms that appeared at the turn of the last century. The same holds good for the development of musical instruments, and even European composers have begun to include South American instruments in their scores. Prokofiev uses the *maracas* in his cantata 'Alexander Nevsky'. In his 'Sacre du Printemps' Stravinsky prescribes the Cuban scraper *guira*. Edgar Varèse in his 'Ionization' uses the Cuban concussion sticks *claves* and the double-membrane drum *bongos* apart from the *maracas* and the *guira*.

THE UNITED STATES
OF AMERICA

The music of the indigenous population of the North American continent died with the virtual extinction of Indians throughout this region. What remained is kept alive artificially here and there rather as a kind of speciality and is far from sufficient to permit the reconstruction of an exact picture of what this music was actually like. On the basis of what has already been said of Mexican and South American Indian music, it may be assumed that the music of the original population of the United States hardly differed from that of the other Indians. A few original melodies preserved among some of the tribes are very simple and almost without expression. Song is usually accompanied by a single-head drum similar to the tambourine. Another kind of drum consists of a hollowed tree-trunk covered with skin at one end. Very rare is the occurrence of that amazing whistle without fingerholes depicted in the Maya annals, in which the air current is brought to the edge opening by a special duct. Rattles made of leather pouches filled with grain or pebbles are used in dances.

The folklore brought from Europe and other continents is much richer. Many nations of the world have contributed to the musical treasure store of North America: the English, French, Italians, Germans, Spaniards, Ukrainians, etc. Their national cultures merged in the melting pot of America and produced new ideas, new national characteristics. The music of the original inhabitants, the Indians, was of slight importance in the development of music in this part of the world. But the music of the American Negroes, directly linked with ancient African cultures, was of great importance. All these influences gave rise to the distinct style of folk music in the USA characterized by its special melody, lively syncopated rhythm and the use of string-plucked instruments as accompaniment.

The king and queen among these instruments are the banjo and the guitar, to be found throughout the entire United States. Originally, of course, neither the banjo nor the guitar looked like the instruments of today. The great-grandfather of the present banjo, the *cora*, is still to be found in Africa, from where it was brought to America. In America itself, in distant corners of the Appalachians, makers of folk banjos are still at work, recalling the prehistory of the present instrument. The *Appalachian dulcimer* is similar to the French folk zither *buche*. It has three metal strings, one for melody, the other two as drone strings, tuned either C, f, c^1, or C, g, c^1. The *Appalachian dulcimer* is also well-known in the north of the United States. In the Appalachians it is used to this day both as a solo and as an accompanying instrument. In North American folklore a large group of bass chordophones is used, from various types of *thumping-sticks* to primitive *contrabasses* with one or more strings, whose origin may often be traced back to Africa.

The *foddletta* played with the foot, is an interesting instrument. The Negro folk singer Jesse Fuller plays the *foddletta* with one foot, and with the other the primitive dulcimer *high hat;* he has a mouth-organ fixed to his chest by means of a special holder and he accompanies his song on a twelve-string guitar. As far as the number of instruments and the difficulty of playing is concerned, Fuller was excelled perhaps only by Norris of Atlanta who considered himself to be a good conductor. Since he could never find an orchestra to conduct, he invented a device by means of which he was able to play six different instruments simultaneously. The range of string instruments and their use is considerable in American folk music. Here, too, is reflected the variety of the musical invention of the Americans who started out with European and other ideas, but managed to evolve amazing musical formations of an entirely new and distinct character.

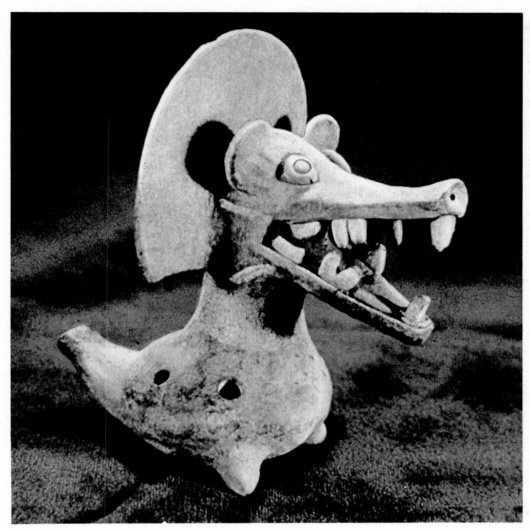

98. Vessel flute *cipactli*
99. Aztec flute *chililihtli*

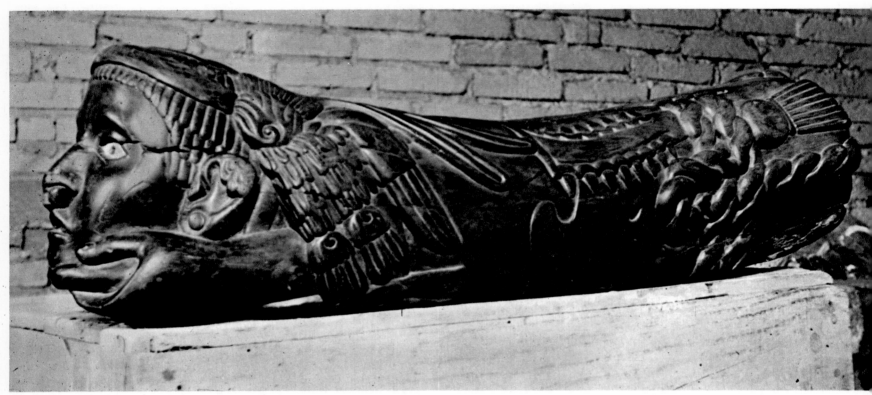

100

101

100.—101. Slit drum *teponaxtli*
of the Maya

102. Single-membrane drum
huehuetl

102

103

103. Mexican pipe and tabor
104. Mexican flautist and drummer

104

105. Mexican guitar players

106. Mexican ensemble of folk instruments

107. Cuban musicians with drums and rattles

108. Cuban drums *bata*

107

108

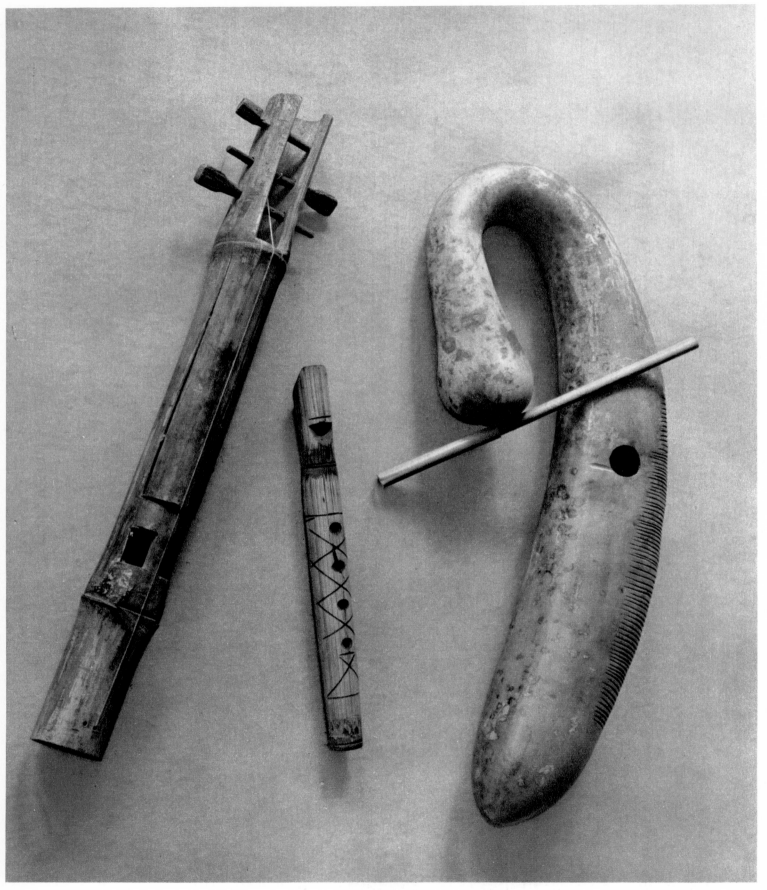

109. Fiddle, flute and scraper from Cuba

110. Panamanian Indians with drums and flute

111. *Marimba* from Guatemala

112

113

114

115

112. Whistling pot *silbador* from Colombia

113. South American bone flute

114. South American pan-pipe

115. Bolivian metal covered horn

116. 'Músicos de madera' (wooden musicians)
from the Altiplana region, Bolivia

117. Bolivian Indians with flutes *ujusinis*

118. Bolivian Indians with horns *pututu*

119. Indian with guitar *charango*

120. Drums of the North American Indians

121. Street musician from the United States

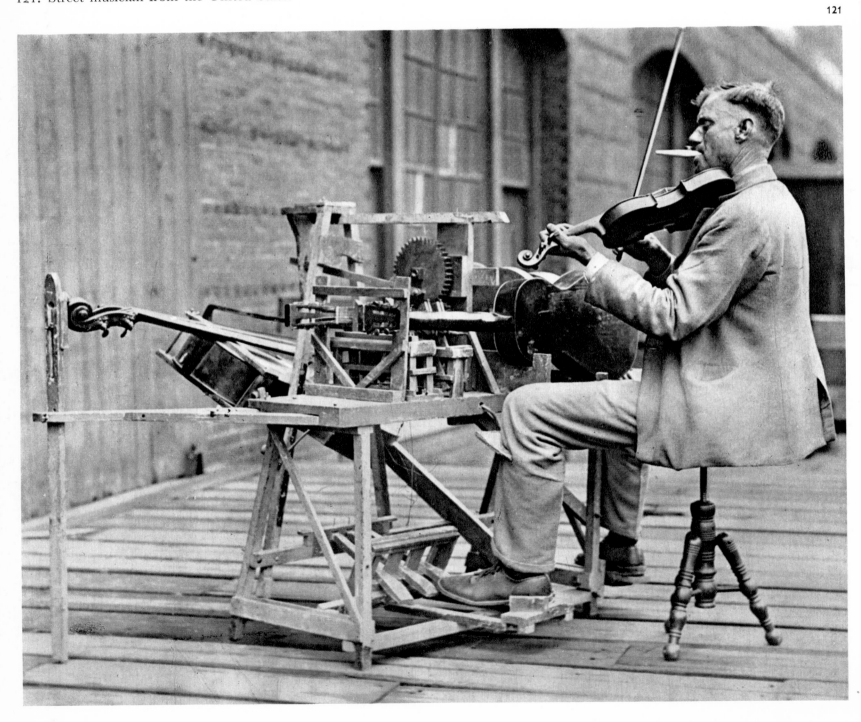

AFRICA

The musical culture of the African continent — inhabited by many races, nationalities and hundreds of different ethnic groups with widely differing cultural traditions — has not by any means been fully investigated as far as the variety of musical forms and styles is concerned. Fairly thorough investigations have been carried out concerning the music of the Arab countries of North Africa and Ethiopia where special literature on musical art exists. The situation is different as far as the music of the peoples south of the Sahara is concerned. However, despite the great differences that exist in the histories of the African nations, certain common features may be observed in their music, features which have often been preserved in some elements of musical practice carefully passed on from generation to generation with amazing exactness. For example, the musicians of the Chopi in Mozambique still tune their xylophones in the same way as the musicians of the Karunga in Southern Rhodesia, a region that the Chopi left more than 450 years ago. Tonometric tests have shown that deviations in tuning do not exceed one-tenth in tone. This refutes the usual statement that African peoples do not possess a well-developed feeling for absolute pitch and that the tuning of their instruments is a matter of chance.

The tonal basis of Negro music is the pentatonic scale, though in the musical practice of various African peoples six- and seven-tone systems, close to the diatonic scale are also used. Each ethnic group usually has one permanent tone system with a definite, strictly fixed succession of intervals. There exist monody and polyphony, the latter having arisen in Africa long before any European influence made itself felt. In harmony there are many intervals from the third to the octave. Parallel thirds particularly are frequently used. Apart from its unusually rich rhythmical structure, African music is also very colourful as far as melody is concerned, though this was not admitted till recently. The function of the drums in African music is manifold. Apart from the human voice the drum is altogether the most natural and spontaneous instrument of expression. Only the Europeans regard the drum as an unmelodic dead instrument without any nuances, which is due to its association with military and light music. But African music has shown that the drum is capable of melodic expression, that it has a tremendous range of shades and that it reacts most sensitively to the musician's mood. The pitch of some African drums compasses an octave, depending on the manner and place of striking the membrane. An orchestra made up of such drums has at its disposal a tonal series close to the diatonic scale with a compass of more than two octaves. This means that African drums indeed 'sing' and, what is more, they also 'talk'. And here we find that the term 'musical instrument' is insufficient to describe African drums. The ability of the drums to 'talk' is conditioned by the fact that some languages of the African tribes are tonally semantic. They almost completely lack such means as suffixes, prefixes, etc., and only different pitch distinguishes the meaning of words with the same one-syllabic roots. Such languages possess several pitches, normally distinguishing high, medium and deep. This is the point of contact between music and speech. The nations of Ghana, Togo, Nigeria, the Cameroon, etc., communicate over considerable distances by means of drum 'language'.

Atumpani, fontofrom, and *asafokjen* are some of the names of the speaking drums of the Ashanti and the Eve in Ghana and the Yoruba in Nigeria. All speaking drums fall structurally into two groups. One consists of slit drums made of one piece, the other of membranophones. The language of the drums contains established phrases for current events in the life of the nation such as births, weddings and deaths. Chieftains and outstanding personalities have their own 'drum' names that are inherited from generation to generation. The *ombutu* and the *ongalabi* are two of the great number of speaking drums in Uganda used to call the people to the harvest, or to welcome leaders and guests. One of the functions of the biggest drum, *omubala*, is to count all the thirty tribes of the nation of the Ganda. Every tribe possesses its own name which is expressed in verse. If members of the royal family are present at a celebration, their 'drum' names are announced by the *omubala*. Among the Yoruba of Nigeria an ancient religious rite based on honouring the mythological ancestors has been preserved. Each of the 400 ancestors has his own drum music, a kind of hymn praising and characterizing him. The *laklevu* of Togo, the *gangan* of Nigeria

Player with the xylophone *bala*, Portuguese Guinea

143

and the *dondon* of Ghana are double-membrane 'speaking' drums on which sounds over a considerable compass can be produced. The *kinguvu* in the Congo and the *kiendu* of the Cassai produce four tones. An important place is held by the 'speaking' drums in folk ensembles accompanying dancing. When members of the royal family dance in Uganda, the *miagaro* is used. The dances of the tribal chieftains in Ghana are accompanied by the *bombaa* and the *mpintsin*. During merry-making and festivities in Western Africa the *ompe, boadze osevenji* and *moses* drums are played. But every orchestra must without fail contain one drum called the 'owner' or 'landlord', setting the tone for the entire ensemble. It talks to the dancers and singers, 'explains' what is to be danced and sung. In the schools of Ghana, Nigeria, Guinea and Tanzania the traditional art of drum 'language' forms part of the curriculum and great care is paid to the development of all forms of artistic creation.

Apart from idiophones and membrane drums, friction drums are also known to the peoples of Africa, and are used mainly in fertility rites. The Ba-ila tribe in South Africa uses them during girls' initiation ceremonies. The friction drums have

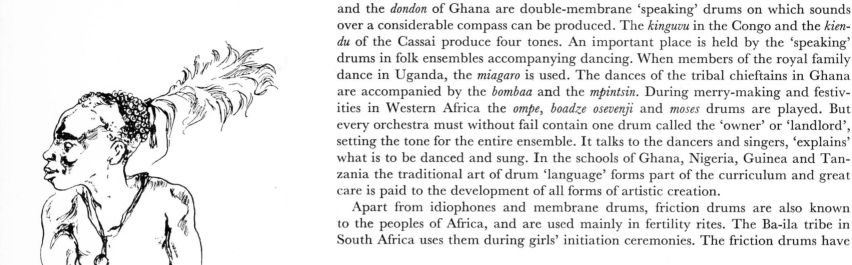

West African tube zither

a string or stick that passes through the centre of the membrane. Sometimes the stick is pressed into the centre of the membrane and fixed there without actually piercing it. In most cases the membrane is set in motion by rubbing the string or stick with resin-covered palms of the hand. The shape of the drums is of no importance so that any kind of drum can be turned into a friction drum. Only the Bantus in South Africa have a special earth friction drum : they dig a pit in the ground and cover it with skins that they rub with the fingers and palms.

Certain points of contact may often be found between the melodic elements of African music and that of the American Indians. This can be seen in the imitation of bird song, animal calls, the whistling and humming of the wind, the murmuring of water and the clap of thunder in close connection with the expression of human emotions: sighing, weeping, laughter, etc. Points of contact are also evident in the construction of the musical instruments of which the most characteristic is the musical bow called *amzad, to*, etc. in North Africa, and *hunga, mtangala, ndimga, nkwindi,*

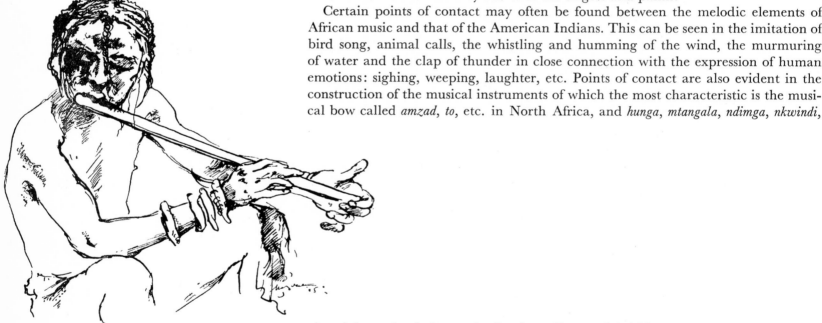

Cross-flute player from Portuguese Guinea

Song accompanied by musical bow

alem, bobre, gubo, hade, etc. in Southern Equatorial Africa and *zhezhilava* in Madagascar. Its age is sufficiently confirmed by the wall painting from the Trois Frères cave near Montesquieu, France from the Magdalenian period shown on the title page of this book. So far scientists have not been able to agree on the origin of this chordophone which is still in use in many continents and which is undoubtedly the oldest instrument of its kind. Curt Sachs' view that the musical bow could not have possibly developed from the hunting bow is refuted by the great expert on South African music Percival R. Kirby, who has definitely ascertained that the bushmen of the Kalahari desert use the hunting bow also as a musical bow. The chord of the hunting bow of the bushmen in South Africa, under favourable circumstances, i.e. when it is plucked under full tension, does produce a tone, the fourth and ninth aliquot tone in particular, with the bushmen using their mouths as resonators. This reveals two more important aspects : firstly, that musical instruments developed from objects of daily use, and secondly that aliquot tones were known and used in a practical way by man from the beginnings of history. Very soon the musical bow became the instrument for magicians' rites and talks with the spirits because of its 'chamber sound'. Its soft, vague sound is also reflected in the dark vowels and nasals of the native names, such as *kalumbu* in northern Rhodesia, *nkungu* in Angola and *wuru-bumba* in the Congo.

Some African instruments permit the performance of solo harmonious music even though harmony in African music is only a means of embellishment or variation of the theme. The most perfect of them is the *sansa (zanza)* (tribes speaking Bantu also call it *usimbi;* in northern Rhodesia it is called *kankobele*, in the Congo *dimba, ekende, ibeka, pokido*, in Mozambique *ambira*, etc.). The *sansa* consists of a number of elastic steel or wood tuned lamellae fitted to a square board or resonator. The tongues are placed over a bridge so that they are free at one end and can be repressed and released by the musician's thumbs. Lyrical compositions for the *sansa* that usually include vocal parts constitute some of the most sophisticated works of African music. Sixteenth-century explorers compared the *sansa* players to European dulcimer virtuosi.

Xylophone orchestras exist in many regions of Africa. In South Africa there are ensembles of bamboo and wooden flutes. The leader of the ensemble plays the main theme, embellishing it with melismatic variations while the other musicians provide the counterpoint basis by the constant repetition of the theme. The xylophone (also *marimba*), which among the African peoples has hundreds of different names, (in Uganda *akandinda*, in Ethiopia *ambira*, in Mali and Guinea *bala*, in the Sudan *balafo*, in Sierra Leone *balangi*, in the Congo *kalanbe, ilimba, baza, dimba*, in South Africa *dipela* or *mbila*, in West Africa *handja*, etc.), is of Malayan origin. It possesses a number of tuned wooden slabs, each of which is supported at two nodal points of vibration. They are struck with sticks. The xylophones of the Bantu people, living in practically all of Africa south of the Equator, usually have a gourd resonator under every slab which is carefully cut in such a way that the air content increases the vibration of the slab as much as possible. An opening is cut in the gourd and covered with a spider's egg membrane to produce a longer and more sharply timbred tone.

Africa offers a rich field of activity to the organologist since, apart from the most primitive sound instruments (scrapers, rattles, thumping pits, ribbon-reeds etc.) there are also more complicated types of self-sounding and string instruments (xylophones, harps, etc.). It is impossible to describe them all in this book. Not every tribe has the same rich armoury of instruments. The Kindig of East Africa have no other instruments apart from rattles, but they whistle and clap their hands. Many tribes prefer indefinite humming sounds to pure tones. The Ganda and Nyoro tribes of East Africa let the strings of their instruments vibrate together with rings of lizard skin fixed at the required distance from the strings on the neck of the harp. These rings may be shifted. The Soga tribe use spherical rattles, usually two in number, for this purpose filled with dried seed and pierced by a hook-like mallet. One musician plucks the strings, the other drums on the resonance lid of the instrument. To obtain supplementary rustlings, rattles (nutshells, pebbles, beads, seeds, etc.,) are fixed also to other types of instruments such as drums, *sansas*, musical bows, etc. The famous ground harp was brought from Africa to Latin America. In the Sudan, Uganda and some parts of East Africa the bowl lyre is to be found in the shape of the ancient Greek pluriarc *kissumba* (in Nubia the *gezarke*) with a semicircular gourd resonator or leather-covered wood from which two wooden sticks protrude joined at the ends by a transverse bar. The guitar-like *wambi* (in the Congo *ndona, ndjembo*, in East Africa *angra, okwena*, in Nigeria *ubo*) has a box-like resonator from which six elastic lamellae protrude keeping liana strings in constant tension.

A primitive wind instrument of the African continent is represented by the bull-roarer (called *burubush* by the Korana Hottentots of South Africa, *seburburu* by the Chwana, *adya-oro* by the Ibo of Nigeria, etc.) which consists of a thin piece of wood attached to a string passed through a small hole pierced at one end and whirled through the air. While being whirled the piece of wood turns on its own axis and the

SANSA

XYLOPHONES

Song accompanied by *sansa*

145

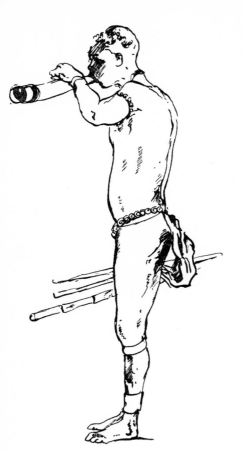

Ivory horn *apunga*, Congo

resultant noise is like the howling of the wind. The smaller the wood and the faster the movement, the higher the sound. Typical wind instruments are ivory horns or antelope horns (in Angola called *apunga* or *mpungi*, in the Western Sudan *burife*, in the Congo *mbuchi* and *nzogh akom*), which instead of a mouthpiece at the end of the tube have a lateral opening like the cross-flute. Their terrifying sound accompanies the rites of the medicine men. The marine-shell trumpet *antsiva* is used in Madagascar during practically all ceremonies, including important family events such as the raising of the dead, healing the sick, boxing contests, etc.

There is no doubt that the African people will succeed not only in preserving but also in further developing their music tradition. The first promising steps have already been made: Lamine Touré, a young musician and expert on West African folklore, has founded an ensemble from the dancers and musicians of seven African states from the Senegal to the Cameroon, with the aim of presenting to the world the music and dances of the African people. Similar ensembles have been founded in other African countries, Guinea and Ghana, for example. The foundations have also been laid for the study of the music of the African peoples. Kwabena Nketia's book *African Music in Ghana* fills one of the many gaps still existing in our knowledge of African music.

ETHIOPIA

The music and musical instruments of Ethiopia have since time immemorial developed under the influence of Arabic-Muslim culture. Many instruments have retained their archaic form to this day. Accompaniment to liturgic song is provided by wind, string and percussion instruments, of which the sistrum *(tsnasin* in Ethiopia*)* recalls its ancient Egyptian predecessors. It is horseshoe-shaped and to symbolize the Holy Trinity three rattling metal discs are suspended from three wires. Silver *tsnasins* are presented to churches by high officials and their tinkling reminds one of the sound of the Mass bells in Catholic churches.

The kettle drum *nagarit* plays an important part both in religious as well as secular life. Only the Church and members of the Sovereign's court are entitled to use it. There are strict regulations according to which the *nagarit* must be made : of silver for the Emperor, of copper for high officials, and of wood for lower officials. The number of drums used also depends on the person's rank. The Emperor is entitled to eighty-eight during military parades. They are the insignia of his dignity and often bear names like the Lion, the Bear, etc. Court officials have a far smaller number of drums. The trumpet *malakat*, with a long skin-covered bamboo tube and fitted with a tuning hole near the mouthpiece, is also a royal instrument. The copper bell is adorned with engravings. The whistle flute *galla* (also called *embilita*) with seven fingerholes is reserved for court officials. The large two-headed barrel drum *kabaro* is a ritual instrument held in high esteem and often hung with precious materials. The *tilik abero* is a Christian ritual drum.

The *sand drum* is a very rare instrument and occurs in the province of Wollo, only found elsewhere among the pygmies of New Guinea. This consists of a small tunnel dug into the earth with two covered openings and a bridge of sand that is beaten with the hands. The pellet-bell drum *atamo*, the sounds of which are supposed to have healing effects, must be included among folk instruments; also the bamboo flute *lemana* used by the Galla tribe, a kind of Arab flute called *naj zagu*, the shawm *vachent*, the cow or antelope horn *quand* and the bagpipe *nibiles*. A variation of the Arabic *rabab*, the bowed *massaneqo*, is the instrument of folk singers. Dirges and religious songs are accompanied by a huge string instrument *bagana* (recalling the old Egyptian and classic lyre) that is up to one metre long and which in Ethiopia is regarded as a copy of David's harp. A smaller variation of the lyre is the *kissar* or *kerar*.

Many young Ethiopian musicians have in recent years attempted to revive the distinct features of national music even though the court and military music created by the Emperor following European styles has its European repertoire and European instruments. The music of the people continues to retain its distinct features and it would be impossible here, for lack of space, to enumerate all the instruments used.

Harp-lute *kasso*, Gaboon

147

Congo dance accompanied by scrapers, drums and double bell after a woodcut, 1678

122

123

122. Rattles from the northern Congo

123. Rattles from Ubangi Shari (Congo)

124

125

126

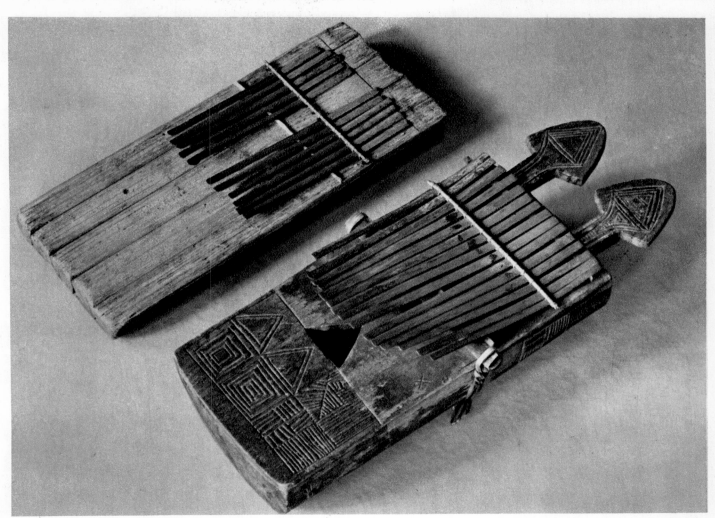

127

128

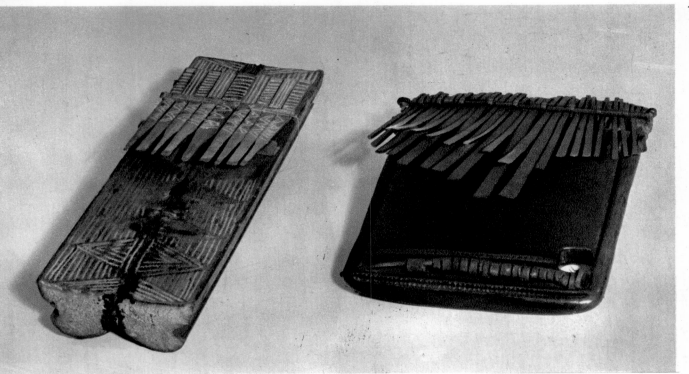

124. Nigerian clappers and gourd rattle

125. Congolese double bell

126. Nigerian gourd rattle

127. *Sansas* from the Cameroon

128. *Sansas* from the Cameroon and South Africa

129

130

131

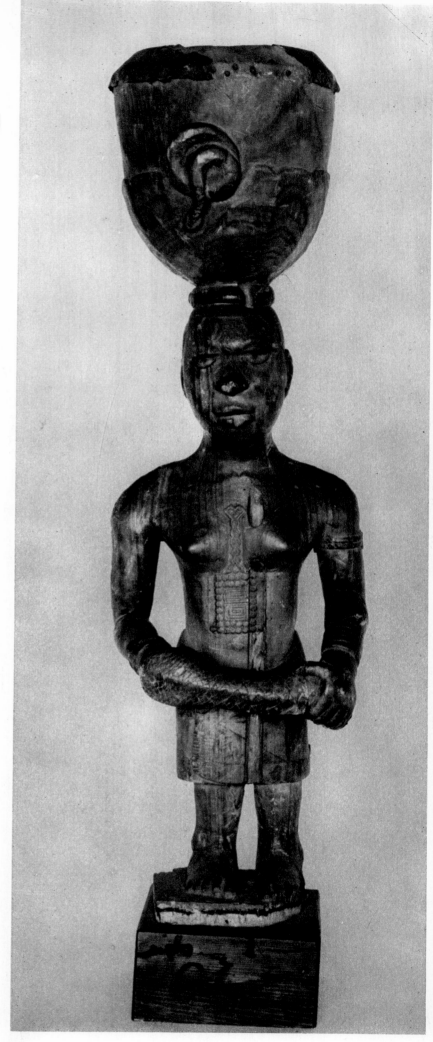

129. Friction drum from Northern
Rhodesia

130. Congolese slit drum

131. West African single-membrane drum

132. Drum on the head of a statuette
from the Central Congo

132

133. Congolese drummer

134. Nigerian single-membrane drum

135. Somali kettle-drum

136. Nigerian 'speaking drum' *kalangu*

137.—138. Single-membrane drums from the Ivory Coast

133

134

135

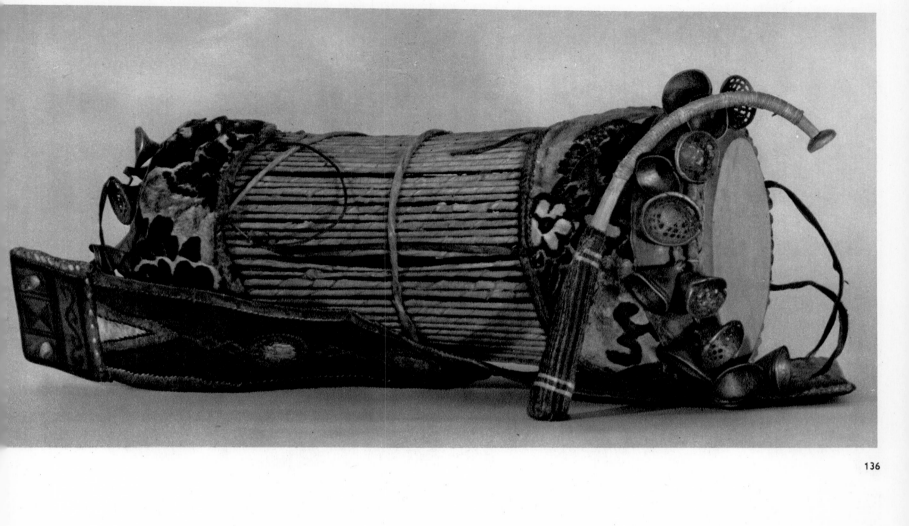

136

137

138

139.—140. Drummers from Dahomey

141.—142. Nigerian drummers

141

142

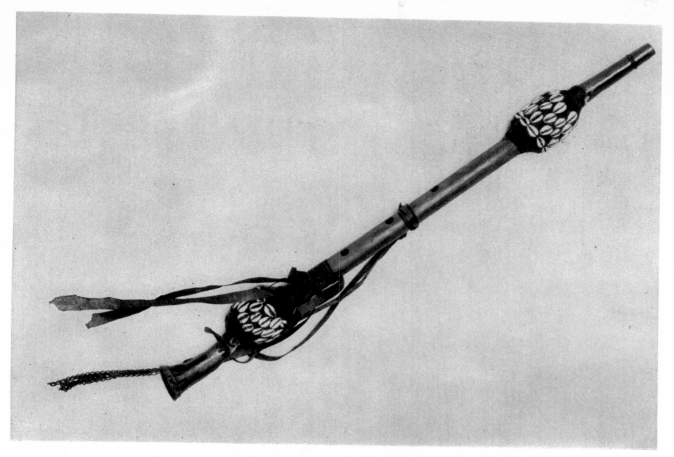

143

143. Nigerian flute

144. Bone flute from British Guiana

144

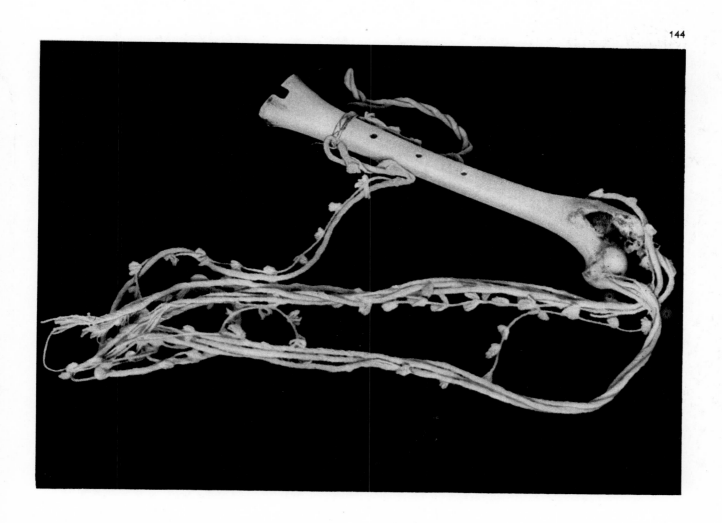

145. Ethiopian shepherd with end-blown flute

146. Crowd surrounding a drummer in West Africa

147. Ethiopian drums *nagarit* and rattles *tsnasin*

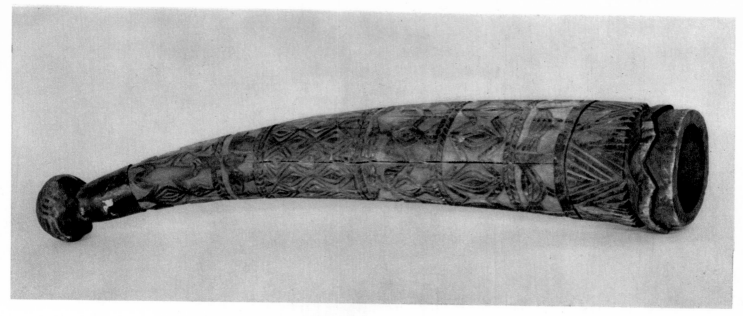

148

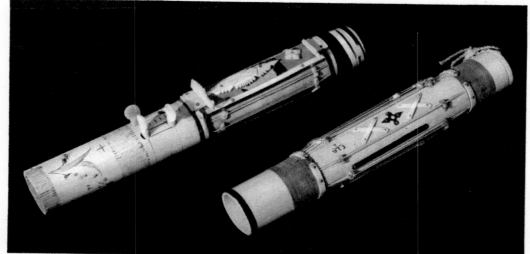

148. Wooden horn from
West Africa

149. Tube zithers *valiha*
from Madagascar

150. Angular harp from
Gaboon

149

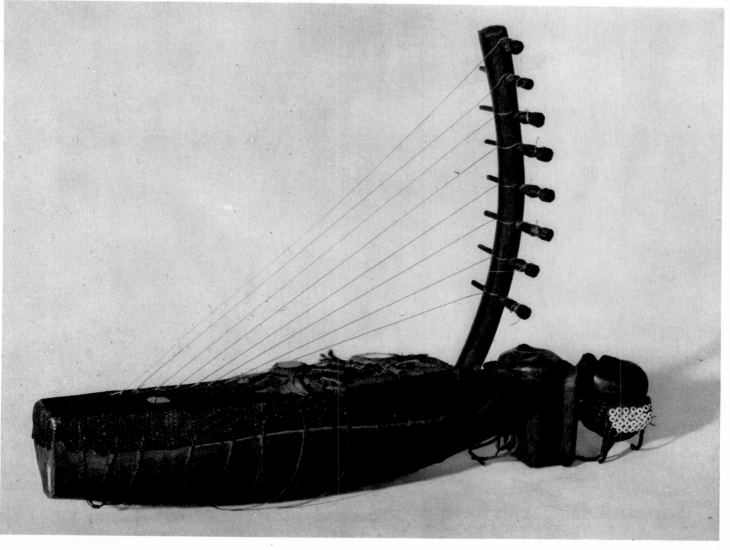

150

153

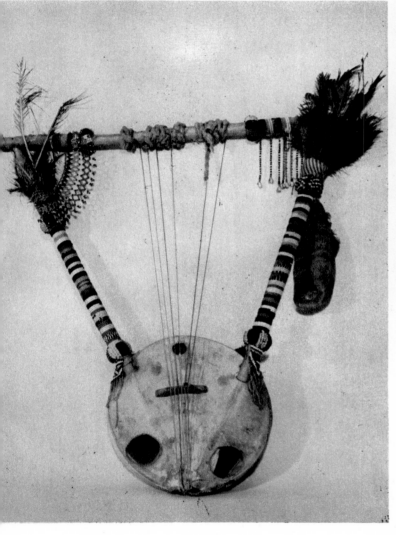

152

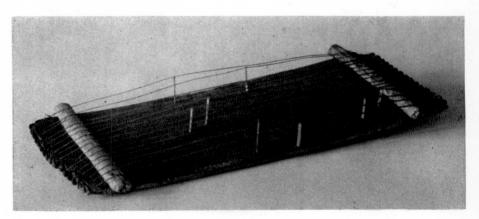

154

151. Scroll of the angular harp from Gaboon

152. Lyre from Uganda

153. Musician from Gaboon with angular harp

154. Congolese zither *totombito*

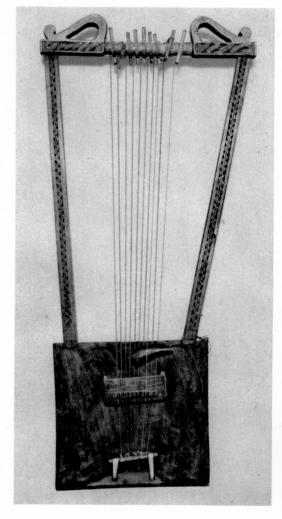

155. Musician playing the lyre (Kenya)

156. Ethiopian lyre *bagana*

157. Iranian harp and drum

158. Goblet drum *darboka* from Tunis

ARABIC
COUNTRIES

The coastal regions of the Mediterranean as early as the first millenium of history became the meeting place of many faces, many peoples. Their relations, whether friendly or hostile, mutually influenced development of their cultures.

Arabic music may be traced from the time when the Queen of Sheba visited King Solomon. Reference to this music and to the instruments used is made in the *Arabian Nights* when the princess orders her slave to bring some musical instruments and she 'returned immediately with a Damascene lute, a Persian harp, a Tartar whistle and an Egyptian dulcimer'.

Persian musical culture left the deepest traces on Arabic music, not only in the development of musical theory but also in the construction of instruments. The most important instrument of Arabic music is the lute *'ud*, which is of Persian origin. Under Iranian influence a seventeen-tone system was created for the *'ud* and the tonal system of the old Arabic (Baghdad) *tanbura* evidently changed. The foundations of the Persian musical system were laid between the third and seventh centuries when court music developed and many foreign musicians performed there. With the hoisting of the green flag of Mohammed over the caliphates of the faithful, national frontiers disappeared as far as musical instruments were concerned. The bowed *kemanje (kemence)* of Kurdistan reached not only the Egyptian story-tellers and ballad singers, but also the Javanese *gamelan*. The *tamburina* of Ethiopian origin accompanied the dances of Algerian and Spanish maidens, and the sound of the Persian shawm *zurna* could be heard among the Dayaks on Kalimantan as well as in Morocco.

Modern Arabic musical theory divides the octave into twenty-four parts, i.e. into quarter-tones. The scale may start at any quarter-tone and is made up approximately of three-quarter and four-quarter intervals, but there are also one-, two-, five-, and six-tone intervals. The system contains a tonal series with the compass g-g^2 and is made up of three-quarter and four-quarter tones interspersed with tones with still smaller intervals, so that the octave always consists of altogether twenty-four tones. These tonal series are not only scales, however, but melodies of the same line. A further distinction is made between the main *makamat*, or 'fathers', always containing only three-quarter and four-quarter tones, and subsidiary *makamata* or 'sons', based on a free sum of one-, two-, five- and six-quarter tones. Exact observations of even the slightest shades in the melodic steps are made possible by the long-necked *tanbur* which, with its twenty-four frets, is a perfect embodiment of the Persian-Arabic musical system.

TONAL SYSTEM

The symbol of the classic Arabic musical theory and the decisive factor in Arabic musical life is the lute *'ud*. There is much discussion among scientists concerning its origin. It is certain, however, to have existed as early as the orchestra of the Han dynasty (206 BC-AD 220). The Arabic name of the lute means flexible rod and this is the reason why it was assumed to have developed from the musical bow. Countries to the west of the United Arab Republic prefer the name *kvitarah*, taken from the ancient Greek *(kithara)*. In shape the lute then resembled the present Chinese and Japanese lute rather than the Arabic instrument. Four drone strings symbolized the elements, the phases of the moon, the points of the compass, the seasons, weeks of the month, division of the day, the human body and life. The silk strings of the lute were plaited similarly to the strings of the Chinese zither *tsisiantsin* always from threads decreasing in number in the ratio 3:4, i.e. 64, 48, 36, 27, etc. The *kvitarah* of today has a neck as long as the body, is played with a plectrum of eagle feathers held between the thumb and two fingers. The instrument is held horizontally in the left hand with the top facing the listeners.

CHORDOPHONES

Beside the *'ud* there appeared in the Islamic Near East a short lute cut from one piece of nut-wood, with a short neck. This instrument spread from Persia further to the east to Sulawesi and south to Madagascar, and also to the west, to Europe, where it reached Central Europe via Moorish Spain under the name of *koboz*. At home the technique of playing the short lute changed from plucking to the use of a bow and under the new name *rabab* two types developed: in north-west Africa an instrument with narrow, piriform body and a parchment-covered belly, and in the United Arab Republic of trapezoid shape, with wooden corpus and parchment belly and back. Both types have two strings, but if the *rabab* of the United Arab Republic has only one string, it is called *rabab ashshair*, which means the 'poet's fiddle'. For the Arabs preserved their love and admiration of poetry. Even a simple nomad will listen with great concentration to a good narrator accompanied by the *rabab*. The two-stringed *rabab* is called *rabab al mogamu*, i.e. 'the singer's fiddle'. Arab songs are actually poems set to music and accompanied by the 'singer's fiddle'. The performance is always watched with great attention on the part of the audience and every part of the production rewarded with loud cries of 'Allah', and expressions of admiration.

At the beginning of the century attempts were made to use European notation for the plucked chordophone *tar*. Iranian musicians favour extensive unison forms called *mahama*, some kinds of instrumental suites containing several movements in a certain scale with great variations in rhythm and speed. The *tar* is mainly used as accompaniment and so is the bowed *kemanje* to be found throughout the Islamic world. These spike fiddles of Persian origin spread as far as Vietnam and Cambodia. The *kemanje* has already been described elsewhere, but from the viewpoint of the Arabic armoury of instruments it must be added that this instrument has survived in many varieties and different tunings. As with Arabic instruments, the zither *kanun (qanun)* (from the Greek *kanon* = rule) reached Europe via Spain and there under the name *canon* or *micanon* played an important part in medieval music. The Arabic *kanun* has a flat resonator, the right side cut at an angle of about forty-five degrees. Twenty-six metal strings in courses of three are led parallel across the tailpiece to the left end, which is rectangular, across the bridge on the right and the pegs fitted at the edge of the cut side of the instrument. They are tuned diatonically with a compass of c^1-g^3. Since it is necessary to retune the instrument for every scale, all strings of three are fitted with a device enabling them to be lowered or raised by a quarter tone. The instrument is played with plectra slipped over the index fingers. The Persian *santir* (from the Greek *psalterion*) has a trapezoid body with eighteen drone strings in courses of four which are struck with light mallets. The *santir* reached central and south-east Europe in the Middle Ages via Spain. It is still found there under the name of dulcimer. The *santir* was confirmed in Korea as early as the eighteenth century, from where it continued to China and Japan.

AEROPHONES

An instrument common to both Arabic and Turkish music is the endblown bamboo flute *nay (nay* = wind instrument) open at both ends with five to six fingerholes. Since the *nay* possesses neither beak nor notched mouthpiece it is extremely difficult to play. To simplify playing some types have a rear thumbhole dividing the vibrating air current exactly into half. The tones of the basic octave would sound too weak on the *nay*, which is why its scale begins with the harmonic octave. To permit the use of the *nay* as an accompanying instrument for the almost endless number of different Arabic scales, it is produced in seven tunings. Another bamboo flute, the *kasbah*, one of the main instruments of folk music in North-West Africa, also indicates that Arabic music absorbed foreign elements. In shape and technique of playing the *kasbah*, whose Berber name is *arhanym*, is sister to the *nay*. Among the Bedouins, the bearers of the simplest but most attractive Arabic tradition, the *kasbah* has three fingerholes.

The Arabs have two shawms, the *zamr* and the *gaita*. The *zamr* has a conical turned pipe and flared bell. The double reed is mouthed entirely, the mouth forming a kind of resonator. The player breathes through the nose while playing, producing uninterrupted sound. In Tunis and Algiers the *zamr* is represented by an instrument identical with the Egyptian *zummarah*, the two pipes of equal length being provided with fingerholes. The player always blocks two opposite fingerholes simultaneously. There are six in each pipe. A similar instrument called *aghanin* with the reed made of split bamboo leaves is played in Morocco. In construction and technique of playing the *gaita* is identical with the *zamr* except that it is a Bedouin folk instrument whereas the *zamr* penetrated higher forms of Arabic music. The double-clarinet *arghul* of the Fellah is of old Egyptian origin. Both pipes are firmly linked to each other and the mouthpiece is formed by two short tubes with a simple idioglot (i.e. the lamella is cut straight out of the tube of the instrument). Only the shorter pipe has fingerholes; the longer is a drone pipe. The three types of *arghul (argul)* differ from one another only in size: *arghul el ashgar* (smaller *arghul*), *arghul el soghair* (medium *arghul*) and *arghul el kebil* (larger *arghul*). Ceremonial processions in Fez — with the exception of the Ramadan — are the only occasions today when the brass trumpet *nefir* can be heard. *Sha nefir* is the name of a spiral-shaped Persian horn. The long metal trumpet *karna* is used in Iraq on festive occasions.

Drums, whose task is twofold, are one of the basic elements in Arabic music. In folk music they set a short unvarying rhythm. In classical music short and long strokes, stressed and unstressed, alternate on percussion instruments within one beat in a strictly determined order. This alternation of rhythmical motifs in a certain, previously chosen rhythm is closely connected with the melody that creates a number of variations on the given rhythmical basis. Without perfect drum accompaniment such a complicated rhythmical structure of melody would be practically impossible. Three types of drums are used in Arabic countries: frame, goblet and kettledrums. The small frame drum *tar* with rattling discs is held in the left hand while the player strikes it with the fingers of the right, alternating between centre and rim. Here the large frame drum *bendir (girbal)* must be mentioned, with an opening in the frame for the player's left thumb, and snares touching the membrane from inside. The instrument is held in the left hand which also beats the subsidiary rhythm while the right hand plays the main rhythm. The *darboka (darbuk, darabuka)* is a goblet-shaped drum, held by the neck under the left arm. The corpus has a membrane instead of a base with two snares. The *darboka* is a favourite with the folk musicians, but is also used in classical music. The *naqqara (tabla, tbilat)* consists of two small kettledrums tied together and beaten with sticks. A folk variant of this instrument is called the *gesah*. The drum *tabl baladi* has given its name to an ensemble made up of the *tabl baladi*, the *naqqara* and two larger and one smaller shawm, *gaita*. The *tabl baladi* recalls the European drum by its low cylindrical corpus and the way in which the membrane is stretched by lacings.

The Arabic armoury of instruments is not rich in idiophones. The cymbals *snug (sunuj, nuviksat)* are played as follows. Two are held in the right hand, and a single one is held in the left and used to strike the other two. Instead of the gong the Copts use the *naqus*, a metal clapper, as a liturgical percussion instrument. It consists of a curved piece of iron placed on a support or across the leg, and is struck with two metal rods. And lastly, the *qaraqib (qaragib, qarabu)* represents a kind of saucer-shaped metal castanets.

Arabic classical music was divided into eastern and western by historical events and differing development, but folk music has remained the same. Wherever it is played today there is an orchestra composed of frame drums *tar*, some small kettledrums *naqqara*, and a lute or a *rabab*. The singer, usually unaccompanied, sits while singing, a faraway look in his eyes, his head resting in his hand. The musician sits facing him, every now and then playing a few quiet notes on the *'ud* or the *rabab*. As soon as the melody has been sung it is taken up by the instruments so that a kind of musical 'dialogue' unfolds between the singer and the instruments that gradually reveals all the features of the melody. The drums participate at the beginning with slight irregular beats and the clanging of the jingles. All this heightens the dramatic effect and only in the intervals might you hear the listeners murmur the name of Allah in praise. But suddenly the singer, together with the instruments, starts again in strict rhythm, once more performing the song already known in text and music. Tension is relieved; the melody is at first heard slowly, but gradually both speed and volume increase only to stop suddenly under the thundering beating of the drums.

MEMBRANOPHONES

IDIOPHONES

173

It is said that when listening to the masterly performance of some musicians, one caliph in the eighth century was so carried away that he tore off his clothes and threw himself into a perfumed bath to cool off. Western musicians insisted that the Moors lost Granada and thus the whole of Spain because they were obsessed by music and ignored their enemies' attacks.

Moroccan player with *rabab*

TURKEY

The historical development of Turkish music has not been investigated yet and all that is known about it is that it is a characteristic variant of Persian-Arabic musical culture. In the course of history Turkey was for a long time not only the bearer of traditional Arabic music, but to a certain extent also further developed, enriched and influenced this type of music. Though the Turks had no outstanding musicologist, apart from Abd el Kadir, a certain manner of classification of musical creation developed. Basically military, folk and religious music is distinguished. And it seems that these kinds are common to both the Islamic centres of musical culture, that of Istanbul and of Cairo. What has been preserved in historical documents and annals of Turkish secular, folk and military music dates from the Hungarian-Turkish wars, when Turkish musical culture made closer contacts with western music. In the sixteenth and seventeenth centuries Turkish folk singers travelled through Hungary and sang their songs to the accompaniment of the *saz*, a long-necked lute. It is not by chance that it was at that time that the *zurna*, the Turkish shawm, spread through Hungary.

A Turkish military band can be found in miniature in Dshelalsades' chronicle depicting the battle at Mohacs (1526). It consists of two folded trumpets *nafir*, three shawms *zurna*, two pairs of cymbals *zil*, two large drums *tabl turki* and in the back-

Turkish army war music during the battle of Mohacs after a miniature by Dshelalsades (16th century)

175

ground two players probably with triangles. All the instruments of this military band were later incorporated into European military bands.

The home-land of Turkish music is Central Asia. This is shown especially by the parlante song material based on pentatonics and confirmed by very old Asia-Minor, Turkish, Turkmenian and Tartar melodies as well as by old Hungarian melodies. Some Mongolian tribes use the drum *bar* during their shamanistic rites, which is the same type of drum as that used by the Turks of Erzerum or Asia Minor. In Trapezunt there exists to this day an instrument called *lyre* which is actually a type of Turkish violin *kemanje (kemence)* and which probably came here via Europe. The *horon*, which is related to it, is by origin one of the ancient folk instruments of the neighbourhood of Trapezunt, a trade centre connecting east and west. The Turkish armoury of instruments mostly includes types already mentioned for the Asian and Arabic peoples. They include the bowed chordophones *kemanje* and *rabab*, the plucked chordophones *'ud, tanbur* and *kanun*, the cylindrical shawm *djudjuk*, the coneshaped shawm *zurna*, the bagpipe *tulumi (gajda)*, the drums *def* and *dumbelek*, etc.

159. Iraqi flautist

160

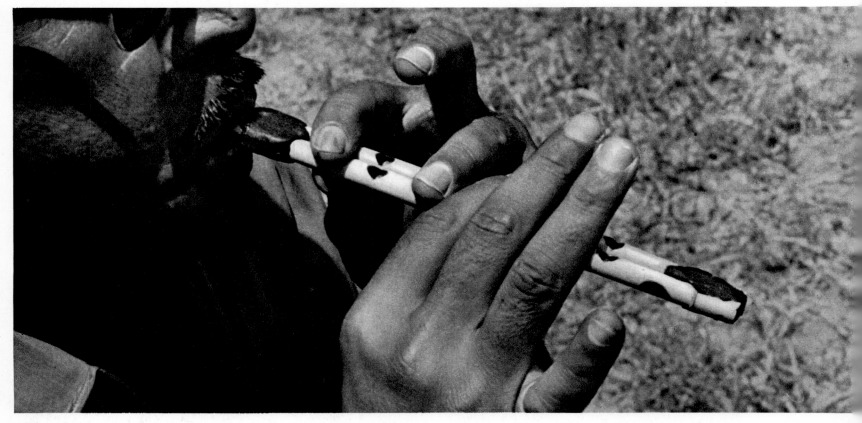

161

160. Syrian musician playing the shawm *zamr*

161. Performance on the Arabic double clarinet *zummarah*

162. Bagpipe *zukra* from Saudi Arabia

163

164

163. Iraqi musician with lute '*ud*

164. Performance on the Arabic zither *kanun*

165. Syrian musician playing the *rabab*

166. Dulcimer *santir* from Iraq

165

166

167

168

167. Double drum *naqqara*

168. Drum from the central Sudan

169. Iraqi musician with the tambourine *bendir*

171

172

170. Tuareg woman with drum

171. Syrian dance with casta-nets *sunuj* accompanied by a lute

172. Beggar from Tunis with *rabab*

173

174

175

173. Performance on the Arabic drum *darboka* (*deblek*)

174. Iraqi drum *darboka*

175. Turkish drum *deblek*

176. Persian drum *darabukke*

177

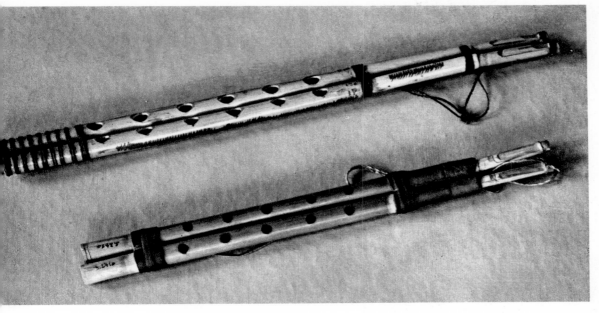

178

179

180

177. Turkish metal flute *sari maden çaval*
178. Arabic double clarinets *zummarah*
179. Turkish musician playing shawm *zurna*
180. Turkish boy with flute *dillidüdük*

182

183

181. Turkish chordophone *saz* (*baglama*)

182. Turkish spike fiddle *kabak kemanje*

183. Turkish zither *kanun*

184

184. Goblet drum *deblek* from southern Turkey

THE SOVIET UNION

The nations living in the extensive territory of the Soviet Union in Europe and Asia have in the course of the centuries created their own musical culture. Their musical instruments include all kinds from the most primitive to the most sophisticated. Despite this great variety they may be divided into five main groups, according to regions.

FAR-EAST
AND NORTH-EAST SIBERIA

After the Huns, the Uighurs, Kazakhs and other tribal unions there lived in the twelfth and thirteenth centuries, in the region of Lake Baikal, Mongolian, Turkish and Tungus tribes that were subjugated to the Mongolian Empire. Later these tribes developed into the Buriat nation. Their folk music is based on a pentatonic scale with idiosyncratic melodic features. The most common instruments are the *khur* (*chur*), *khuuchir* and the *limba*. The bowed *khur* with two strings is identical to the Mongolian *morin khuur*. Folk songs are accompanied by the bowed *khuuchir* of Mongolian-Chinese origin with oval corpus covered with snakeskin and two drone strings tuned a, d^1. The *limba* is a bamboo cross-flute with seven fingerholes. Among the western Buriat Mongolians the *limba* is replaced by the end-blown flute *sur*. The shawm *bishur* is similar to the Uzbek *surnaj*. The plucked chordophone of Chinese origin *chanza*, with oval snakeskin-covered corpus is the instrument of professional musicians.

BURIAT REPUBLIC

Tuvinian musicians. Left to right: guitar *topshulur*, bowed *pyzanchi*, flute *limba*, bowed *igil* and tambourine

The Yakuts live in the main catchment area of the Lena River and on the New Siberian Islands. After shamanism disappeared the tambourine *dyungyur* was no longer used and today not even the drum *dolyokkyoy kyupsyur* is played. The songs of the folk singers of the Olonchosuts are accompanied by the chordophone *kyryppa* (from the Russian *skripka* = violin) made from any material at hand. Four strings tuned in unison and octave are retuned for every song, for the musicians of Yakutsk insist that every song needs its own tuning. The women play the metal Jew's harp *chomus* (*khomus*), singing at the same time in rather a guttural manner. This produces a characteristic sound effect referred to as 'talking' *chomus* (*khomus*).

CENTRAL ASIA

KAZAKHSTAN

More than a hundred nations live in the territory of Kazakhstan situated between the lower reaches of the Volga and the Chinese border, of whom the original inhabitants, the Kazakhs, today hardly form thirty percent. The folk singers 'anshi' accompany their songs on the *dombra* with the corpus made of one piece. It has a long neck and small shovel-shaped scroll. The bowed *kobyz* shaped like a ladle also has a corpus made of one piece. The player rests the instrument on the floor or against his knee and plays simultaneously on both strings tuned in fourths in a flageolet technique, playing the melody on the first string and the accompaniment on the second in parallel fourths or fifths. The shepherd's instrument is an endblown flute *sybyzgi* with four to six fingerholes. The Kazakh Jew's harp *komyz* or *temir-komyz* is favoured by women and young people. The kettle-drum *daulpaz* used to be tied to the saddle and played in war or during hunting. Today the *daulpaz* is part of the state ensemble of musical instruments.

Kurmangazy: composition for *dombra* (fragment)

KIRGHIZ REPUBLIC

The first reports of the Kirghiz living in the Central Asian massif of Tchien-shan date from the first century BC. They are the descendants of tribes that lived on the Upper Yenissei. Up until the Great October Revolution Kirghiz music existed only in oral folk creation kept alive by the folk musicians. Before that time the Kirghiz did not know choral singing, orchestral music, dancing or dance music. As in ancient times you can still hear today, in the villages on the grey summits of Tchien-shan, the *komuz* with three strings tuned in various ways but always so that the central string is tuned higher than the other two. The outer strings are tuned a fourth and a fifth apart from the central string, which means that two- and three-note chords may be produced and melodies accompanied in parallel fourths and fifths. The bowed two-string *kiyak* with flat, elongated corpus is similar to the Kazakh *kobyz*. From the other instruments two types of open flutes are used: the wooden *choor*, and the brass *sarbasnay* with four front fingerholes and one rear thumbhole. The Kazakh women, like the Kirghiz women, enjoy playing the wooden or metal Jew's harp *temir-komuz*.

Fragment of folk melody for the Kirghiz *komuz*

Many cultures have intermingled in the territory between the Aral and the Caspian Sea to the west and the mountain barriers of Tchien-shan to the east, between the South Siberian steppe and the highlands of northern Persia and Afghanistan. This is as far as Alexander the Great got on his gigantic march from Greece to India. His successors left the mark of European culture on Central Asia. With the advance of Buddhism at the beginning of our era Indian influence became very strong.

Depictions of musicians and musical instruments on silver dishes from the third century BC, terracotta figurines of musicians with their instruments discovered in the small town of Ayrtam, and treatises on music by world-famous Central Asian scholars (Alfarabi, Ibn Sina, Dzhami, etc.) speak of the rich heritage of the Uzbekh and Tadzhik peoples. In the rich armoury of instruments first place is held by the two-string *dutar* with piriform corpus glued from bent strips of mulberry wood. The tapering neck has thirteen or fourteen frets. The strings are most often tuned in the fourth D-G, sometimes in unison, and the fifth. Great vocal and instrumental works called *makoma* are accompanied on the three-string plucked *tanbur* which, as to construction, tuning and manner of play, is identical to the *tanbur* of Tadzhikistan. Other variants of the *tanbur* are used by professional musicians, such as the *setar*, *pandzhtar* and *sheshtar*, (in Tadzhikistan the *setor*, *panchtor* and *duvozdator*), differing from one another only by the number of strings. The *setar* has three, the *pandzhtar* five and the *duvozdator* twelve. Both types of *rubab* played in Uzbekistan, i.e. the Afghan (Tadzhik) as well as the Kashgar type, are the same as in Tadzhikistan. This holds good also for the less far-spread *dumbrak* which is identical to the *dumbrak* of Tadzhikistan. The *chang* is a kind of dulcimer with a flat trapezoid box on four legs. The metal strings (except for the deepest which is single) run in courses of three and diatonically tuned. They are struck with light wood or bamboo sticks. The chordophones are supplemented by two bowed instruments, the *gwidzhak* (*ghichak*) and the *kobuz*. The *gwidzhak* agrees structurally with the *ghidzhak* of Tadzhikistan and Turkmenia, i.e. it has a round corpus with membrane belly, a metal bridge and three or four strings tuned in e^1, a^1 and d^2. The *kobuz* is identical to the Kazakh *kobyz* and appears in some parts of Uzbek only.

The flute *naj* shows its Arabian ancestry not only in its name. *Koshnaj* is a wind instrument with two reeds of the same length and seven fingerholes; the *balaban* is similar. After *naj*, the most common instrument is the shawm *surnaj*; its conical pipe is characteristic. The *surnaj* is always played as a solo instrument, which differentiates it from the related *surna*, which is always used in neighbouring countries as a double instrument. The strains of the brass trumpet, the *karnaj*, which can be up to three metres long, used to herald the beginning of a special occasion. Today the *karnaj* is a ceremonial instrument used at parades, processions and folk festivals.

Among the drums, the tambourine *dojra* is common in the whole of Uzbek and Tadzhikistan and practically no ensemble is complete without it. Metal rings hang from the inside of the wooden frame of the *dojra* and the solo player can heighten its effect by using metal tips like fingers. Two small kettle-drums of Persian origin play a similar role to the *dojra* — the *nagora* (from the Persian *naqqara*) which is also called *timplipito* in Tadzhikistan; their tones used to announce the ceremonial approach of the Emirs and Khans. The bass drum *tawljak* is common in the mountain districts of Tadzhikistan. *Kajrak* (in Tadzhikistan *kajrok*) are castanets made from small smooth stones.

The *safail* (*sapai*) is played in the same way as the *kajrak* is in folk music ensembles in Uzbek and Tadzhikistan; there are two wooden sticks on which free hanging metal rings with jingling small rings are tied.

The music of the Turkmenians, which is foremost in the mountain districts of South West Soviet Middle Asia, developed in narrow association with the art of other middle Asian peoples and was spread by the folk singers, the *bachachi*. The number of Turkmenian folk instruments is small, for example up to very recently the Turkmenians did not have any percussion instruments. Contemporary ensembles are now beginning to introduce the drum and the triangle. The *dutar* is one of the instruments more widely used by the folk singers. It is smaller and has a shorter neck than the Uzbek *dutar*. The bowed *ghidzhak* (*ghichak*) is identical to the Caucasian *kemanje*. During open-air folk festivals musicians play the long end-blown flute *kargy-tyuydyuk*. *Dillityuydyuk* is a reed clarinet with three to four fingerholes. By doubling this instrument you get the *gosho-dilli-tyuydyuk*, related to the Uzbek *koshnay*.

Daghestan is the most southerly autonomous republic of the Russian Federation. The make-up of the population is very varied, since it includes eighty-one different nationality groups the largest of them being the Avars, Dargins, Kumyks, and Laks.

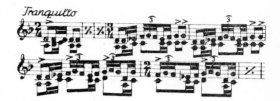

Karakalpaka melody for the dutar

Uzbek musician Mirafgan Akimov with flute *naj*

Uzbek player with trumpet *karnaj*

197

Turkmenian melody for *dutar*

The Kumyks and Dargins have a three-string plucked instrument *agach-komuz* (which the Avars call *tamur*) with the corpus made of one piece in the shape of an elongated shovel and terminating at the lower end in a kind of trident. Tuning differs greatly. It is in fourth, fourth-fifth, or fourth-third. The *tar*, which the Lezgins call *tara*, and the Kumyks and Aktins *chongur* is played in the southern part of Daghestan. An instrument similar to the *saz* of Azerbaijan is called *saaz* by the Tabasarans and Lezgins, *chungur* by the Dargins and *chugur* by the Laks. The bowed *chagana* played among the Avars and Laks is similar to the Georgian *chianuri*. It is a type of spike fiddle similar to the *kemanje* with a flat sheepskin-covered corpus.

All nations of Daghestan have the idioglot *yasti-balaban*, similar to the *balaban* of Azerbaijan, which is made from apricot wood, with eight front fingerholes and one rear thumbhole. The *yasti-balaban* is a solo instrument, but also very suitable for orchestras where it is used to accompany song and dance. The *zurna* is equally widely used differing from the instruments of the same name used in the other Central-Asian countries only in size and the placing of the fingerholes. The accordion is first met as a folk instrument in Daghestan. *Komuz* (*argan* as it is called by the Kumyks) is a type of the so-called Asiatic or 'eastern' accordion, structurally similar to the Vyat accordion from which it differs only in that when extending and compressing the bellows the pitch of the tone does not change. At the present time the *komuz* has become so wide-spread that it must now be regarded as the national instrument of Daghestan. *Gaval* is a double-head drum differently named by each of the nations: *daldama*, *kili*, *dachu*. The girls' choral singing is accompanied by the monotonous beat of the tambourine with jingles *töp* (*zhirkhen*, *dzhirin*, *checheren*, *chchirghilu*). The Georgian clay kettle-drums *diplipito* correspond to the *tiplipitom* of Daghestan. A bell is fixed to them which is occasionally struck by a small stick. Two *yasti-balabans* and a *tiplipitom* form a favourite trio used to accompany dances and solo performances.

The twelfth-century poet Nizami Gandzhevi enumerates more than thirty musical instruments in use in Azerbaijan. The folk singers 'ashug' tell their stories and sing to the accompaniment of a string instrument with long neck *saz*, also called *ashug saz*. The strongly convex piriform corpus of the *saz* is made of mulberry wood. The flat belly has small sound holes sometimes also placed at the side of the instrument. The number of strings varies from four to eight and more and is divided into three groups, melodic, tuning and drone. Fourth-fifth tuning is most frequent, when the melodic strings are tuned one-fourth higher and the drone strings a fifth higher than the tuning strings. This permits an accompaniment in fifth to the melodies played on the upper strings of the *saz*. Together with the *balaban* and the *nagara* the *saz* forms the Ashug vocal instrumental ensemble with a wide repertoire of dance music. The plucked chordophone *tar*, differing from the *saz* in shape and construction, is connected with the development of classical music in the 'mugam' style. The *tar* has an octagonal corpus, the belly covered with the heart membrane of a bull. Strings usually number eleven and are divided into three groups, differentiated by the colours white, yellow and black. They are tuned in pairs and unison, in the first group g, c^1; in the second group one string is tuned in unison with the third pair to c; in the third group four supplementary strings are tuned in pairs in unison to g^1, c^2. The *tar* together with the *kemanje* and the tambourine *dyaf* forms an instrumental ensemble accompanying folk and classical music.

Tutek is a shepherd's whistle flute fitted with a special mechanism to simplify intonation. This consists of an opening and above it a wooden stopper with a lateral slit into which the player blows. *Balaman* and *zurna* are shawms. Usually two players perform on the *balaman* simultaneously, the maestro playing the melody and his assistant accompanying him on the drones. This duo is sometimes supplemented by the cylindrical two-headed drum *nagara* (*bala nagara*), a pair of kettle-drums *gosha nagara* (*dumbul*) and the tambourine *daf*, which in no way differs from the tambourines of the neighbouring peoples.

The plucked chordophone *pandiru* was used by folk musicians of Armenia (situated in the southern part of Transcaucasia) to accompany their songs as early as during the tribal system. In the seventeenth century the activities of the professional folk musicians, the 'gusans' developed widely. In earlier times the 'gusans' wandered from village to village with the *saz* or *kemanje*. Today they most often play on the *kyamani*, a violin with narrow elongated corpus similar to the Italian *sordone*. The other Armenian chordophones originated in the armoury of the ancient Persian-Arabic musical instruments. They include the lute *'ud*, the zither *kanon* and the dulcimer *santur*, mainly used today in the 'gusan' ensemble Sayat-Nova.

The end-blown shepherd's flute *sring* is made either of bamboo or metal. *Blul* has a bell adorned with rings. The bagpipe *parakapzuk* (*tik*) with kid bellows and a pair of reed pipes used to be great favourites in the past but have now become fairly rare. In special string orchestras the clay kettle-drum *nagar* is used and almost all orchestras include the tambourine *daf*. Zurna players are usually joined by a musician playing the two-headed drum *dool*, where one membrane is thicker than the other. Larger *dools* are called *gos* or *kyos*. When playing on both heads the thicker membrane is beaten from above with a thick stick and the thinner one with a thinner stick from below. If the *dool* is played with the hands only, then the right hand plays a lighter rhythm varied in a masterly manner.

The characteristic feature of Georgian folk music (the Georgians live in the western and central part of the Caucasus) is part-music, usually for three voices, the voices alternately taking over the main part. The main instrument of amateur and professional orchestras is the plucked chordophone *panduri*. It is such a favourite that other string instruments are often called by the same name. In shape the corpus of the *panduri* is similar to the *agach-komuz* of Daghestan. Three gut strings are tuned either in seconds or third to g¹, a¹, c², or the two upper strings in unison and the third in octave, i.e. a, a¹, a. There probably does not exist a single village of the Megrels or Guriys where the *chonguri* is not played. This instrument differs from the *panduri* in that it has a slightly shorter but more convex corpus. A fourth, shorter string is added running to the peg at the left in the middle of the neck. The strings are tuned to d, g, b, d¹. The *chonguri* is played mainly by women, as is also the angular harp *changi* with strings plaited from horsehair. Several types of this kind of harp exist, and a great favourite is the six-string *changi*, with three strings tuned in minor (d, f, a) and three in major (c, e, g). Apart from the *kemanje* the Georgians have two more bowed instruments of a similar nature, *chiamuri* and *chunuri*. *Santari* (*cincilla*) is the Georgian dulcimer with drone strings in courses of five and a diatonic compass of three octaves.

Only the older generation still remembers the pan-pipe *larchemi*, made of bamboo whistles with the two longest in the centre. The flutes *salamuri* and *ueno-salamuri* correspond to the end-blown flutes of the neighbouring peoples. The Georgian *duduki* is related to the Armenian *duduk* and the Central-Asian *zurna* corresponds to the Georgian *zurna*. The bagpipe *gudastviri*, the tambourine *doyra*, the clay kettle-drum *diplipito* and the drum *doli*, with two heads, once used to be widespread.

Armenian Gusan Dshiwani with *kyamani*

Georgian Ashug Grikow with lute *saz*

THE AUTONOMOUS
REPUBLICS

ABKHAZIAN AND ADZHAR REPUBLIC

There are many nations living in the Caucasus region to this day that have preserved the characteristics of their national music, as for example, the Abkhaz and the Adzhars. The basis of their folk music is shepherd's songs accompanied on the end-blown flute known as *acharpan* by the Abkhaz and *chaban salamuri* by the Adzhars. Another Abkhaz musical instrument is the bowed spindle-shaped chordophone *apkherca* with the corpus made from one piece. The bowed chordophone *ardanuchi* of the Adzhars resembles the *kyamani* of Armenia. Both nations widely use the Georgian *chonguri* (called *achengur* by the Abkhaz) and the drum *doli*.

NORTH OSSETIA

North Ossetia is an autonomous republic in the north of Georgia. The ethnographer Khetagurov described how some Ossetians played the harp *fandyr* to one of their sick relatives. It is the custom among the people of Ossetia to use the name *fandyr* also in connection with other instruments. The ethnographer Kopyev writes: 'In every house you can see *kisyn fandyr*, which is widespread thanks to its simple construction. You take a wooden goblet to which a wooden board is fixed as a fingerboard parallel with the bottom. The goblet is covered with a membrane, an opening is bored in the bottom of the goblet and several smaller ones in the membrane. Then two strings, a thicker and a thinner one, are stretched.' Today the *kisyn fandyr* has three strings tuned in fourths or fifths. *Dala fandyr* is a three-string plucked chordophone with an elongated shovel-shaped corpus of one piece. The strings are tuned in fourths or fourth-fifths. A special sound effect is used during play, two fingers gliding along the strings, and the belly is tapped. *Duadastanon* (= twelve strings) is a small angular harp which, according to legend, was made by the hero Syrdon from the bones of his elder son's hand and the cardial arteries of his younger sons. A frequently used solo instrument is the end-blown flute *uadynz* with three fingerholes. Apart from boards on which the rhythm is beaten with mallets (as there is a shortage of membranophones) the Ossetians have the clapper *karcganag*, made of rectangular slabs threaded on a string. The only drum in Ossetia is called *gumsag*. Though its cylindrical corpus has two leather-covered heads only one membrane is beaten with sticks. Beginning with the latter half of last century the accordion has begun to be used. It was constructionally adapted to the requirements of folk music and has replaced almost all other instruments. At the present time the diatonic accordion *iron kandzal fandyr*, with twenty melody and twelve bass keys based on the same mechanical principle as the 'eastern' accordion of Daghestan, is widely used.

The Bashkirs have a characteristic flute *kuray* with four front fingerholes and one rear thumbhole. It is made from the reeds of a grass called *kuray*. The kuray player is a respected citizen without whom — and naturally, too, without the folk singer — no celebration used to be complete. The second folk instrument of the Bashkirs is the Jew's harp *kubyz*. Its gentle humming sound is clearly distinguishable during the performances of the Bashkir state dance ensemble.

Only two instruments of the original armoury of the Tatars have survived, the Jew's harp *kubyz* and the flute *kuray*. Both are identical to the Bashkir instruments of the same name. In the course of time the Tatars became familiar with instruments of other nations such as the mandolin *domra* (*dombra*), violin and above all the accordion. At the present time the most widespread type of accordion is the *Italian* (*talianka*) with twelve to twenty keys and one to six chord buttons and the corresponding chords. The harmony in bass is altered by changing the direction in which the bellows are moved. Sometimes there is an extra key placed together with the bass keys producing

Abkhaz player with *apkherca*

200

only one high tone, doubling the dominant on the right keyboard and fulfilling the function of a dominant pedal.

The nature of the Udmurt folklore is due to the combining of the diatonic tonalities taken over from the Russian folksong. Musical instruments include the zither *krez* (*kyrez*) similar to the old Russian *gusle*. *Uze gumy* is a primitive flute without fingerholes and open at both ends. An equally primitive instrument is the *chip-chirgan*, a small reed grass placed into a wooden cone-shaped resonator. The tone is produced by sucking. *Byz* is a pipe with a chanter and a drone whistle. From among foreign instruments the *balalaika* has become a favourite and so also has the accordion *khromka*.

Part-music in diatonic major and minor scales is typical of the folk music of Adygey. The singer is accompanied by a musician on the end-blown shepherd's flute *kamyl* (=reed) which is held in the corner of the mouth in such a way that during playing one tooth (canine) is placed in the tube. The *kamyl* is sometimes accompanied by the two-string chordophone *shichepshin* (*shiche* = horsehair, *pshin* = sound) of the same type as the *apkherca* of the Abkhaz. *Pkhachich* is similar to the Ossetian clapper *karcganag*. It is beaten regularly to set the rhythm for dancing.

In the Kabardinian Republic dance music is played by the angular harp *pshina dykuako* related to the Ossetian *duadastanon*, the two or three-string bowed *shicha pshina* related to the *shichepshin* of Adygey.

Considering vocal genres the instrumental music of the Chuvash Autonomous Republic is less developed. Mostly there exist dance melodies simple in tune and developing mainly by variation. Many folk instruments still exist, partly original, partly taken over. Once the zither *kyosle* (from the Russian *gusle*) was widespread, and is related to the *uze gumy* of Udmurt. The name *sergoch kubos*, used once to refer to an instrument similar to the *kovyzh* of the Mari, now refers to a violin made at home. *Tutut* is similar to the Russian *zhaleyka*, a shepherd's reed instrument producing a sharp, nasal sound, played at weddings together with the bagpipe *shabr*. Of the two drums, the frame-drum *khangrma* and the drum *parappan* with two heads, the latter is more interesting. It is struck with cone-shaped sticks of unequal length. *Vish kides* or *tingeldi* is a metal triangle used most often together with the *gusle* or *parappan*.

The folk music of the Mari Republic makes use of various types of pentatonics. The folk musicians of Mari are most inventive and manage to produce a melody from the leaf of a wild cherry, which is called *lishta*. The musical bow *kon-kon* can still be found, though rarely, in Mari. One end is placed on the lips during play and

UDMURTS

ADYGEY

KABARDINO-BALKARIAN REPUBLIC

CHUVASH

MARI

Chuvash bagpipe *shabr*

201

the string is plucked with the fingers. One of the most frequently used instruments is the *kyusle*, identical with the *kyosle* of Chuvash. The ancient two-string bowed instrument *kovyzh* with oval or rectangular corpus resembling the medieval European *fidula* is more and more frequently replaced by the violin. The recorder *arama shush-pyk* (= wooden nightingale) without fingerholes occurs in the northern districts in contrast to the vessel flute in the shape of a bird or small animal called *shun shushpyk* (clay nightingale). The whistle flute *shialtysh* with cut-back mouthpiece and several fingerholes used once to be a great favourite. It was permitted to play this instrument only between 20 July (Ilja [Elias, Elijah] Day) and 14 September (Raising of the Holy Cross). Only men play the Mari bagpipe *shuvyr*, the bag of which is made from a bull's bladder. It has two chanter pipes. The *shuvyr* is being replaced more and more frequently at weddings by the accordion *koga-karmon* which, together with the double-headed drum *tumyr*, forms a popular duo. When listening to these instruments the audience claps in time with the music and calls rhythmically 'oy-oy-oy-oy'.

RUSSIANS, UKRAINIANS AND BYELORUSSIANS

Frescoes on the staircase of the cathedral of Kiev dating from the twelfth century depict musicians with flutes, cymbals, horns, violins and *kobza*. Pictures and written records of a later date confirm that even then the *gusle*, an instrument with many strings and large corpus enjoyed great popularity. The *gusle* (*gusli*), like a similar instrument of the Baltic nations, the *kantele*, belongs to the medieval group of psalteria. One of the three types of *gusle* is still called *gusli psaltir* (*gusle* psaltery) or *gusle shlemovidnye* (helmet *gusle*). At present it occurs only among the peoples living in the Volga catchment area where it was brought by Russian musicians. The two other types of *gusle* have survived in some outer regions of northern Russia. *Gusle zvon-chatye* (winged *gusle*) is wing-shaped with five to fourteen diatonically tuned strings. *Rectangular* (or table) *gusle* is structurally the most complicated of all types similar to a clavichord in appearance. The large number of strings (up to sixty) used to be tuned chromatically. In 1914 a *gusle* with a keyboard was built, the keyboard not serving to strike the strings but only to release the dampers. Chords are released on the instrument with one hand, while the other hand passes a plectrum of hard leather over the strings. The plucked instruments of the Great Russian region include the *domra*, *bandura* and *balalaika*. Since the *domra* players used to sing ironic and satirical songs often directed against the authorities, it was forbidden to invite them into private homes so that in the course of time the *domra* fell into disuse. It was revived only at the end of the last century. New instruments were built and a whole series of *domras* created from the descant to the bass with three strings tuned in fourths. The *bandura* developed from the *kobza*, an instrument widespread among the Slavonic peoples in the Middle Ages. The present structure and playing technique of the *bandura* recalls the *gusle zvonchatye*. It has thirty and more chromatically tuned strings played with a plectrum fixed to the index finger of the right hand. The *bandura* is the most wide-spread Ukrainian folk instrument which — according to the experts — faithfully portrays the national character of Ukrainian folk music. The *domra* has

Ukrainian *bandura* players

been replaced by the *balalaika* with its typical, triangular corpus, even though *balalaikas* with ovoid corpus exist. Two gut strings are tuned in fourths. If the *balalaika* has three strings, the second and third are tuned in unison. At the end of the last century the *balalaika* was perfected and its various modern sizes established.

In the Smolensk region of Russia the *lira* (Byelorussian *lera*) has been preserved. The Ukrainian *relya* is of similar construction with three gut strings, one melody and two drone. In the Ukraine there used to exist well-attended schools for *lira* players where experienced musicians taught. The construction of the *relya* has considerably improved in the past. A very clever construction is to be found in an instrument with nine strings tuned in small thirds and fitted with a mechanism similar to that of the hurdy-gurdy. The wooden disc which rubs the strings is replaced here with a continuous belt of plastic material whose pressure on the strings can be regulated.

Wind instruments surviving in Central Russia include the pan-pipe *kuvikli* (also *kuvikchi, cevnica*), made up of from two to five whistles of varying length that are not fixed to one another but held freely in the hand during playing. The musician places the separate whistles to his lips and moves them now to the right and now to the left to obtain different tones, supplementing missing tones with his own voice. Every whistle has its own name and various groupings in the hand of the player exist. The complete series consists of five whistles. *Sopel*, corresponding to the Ukrainian *sopilka (dencivka)* and the Byelorussian *dudka* is one of the oldest types of flutes existing among the Eastern Slavs. The tube of the *sopel*, made of maple or nutwood, has five to six fingerholes. Technically it is a very versatile instrument. Apart from the current manner of play the *sopilka* is played in the Ukraine in such a way that the musician lightly covers the sound hole with his lower lip, thus producing a strange gurgling sound. An equally archaic type is the double flute *svirel* called *podvoynaya svirel* (double whistle) in Byelorussia. The whistles are not fixed to each other and during play are held at an acute angle, the longer whistle producing sounds a fourth lower than the shorter whistle. The Ukrainian *dvodencivka* (double whistle), made of one piece of wood with joint beaked mouthpiece, differs somewhat from these two double flutes. In the western Ukraine, the Huculs *telenka*, a flute without fingerholes, and *floyara* (in the east *zubovka*), a block flute with six fingerholes, are especially popular. The *gusle* and accordion are usually combined with the *zhaleyka (bryolka)*, an instrument occurring in northern Russia and Byelorussia, with a reed either inserted into the mouthpiece or carved directly from the pipe. Since it has a bell made from a cow's horn (Russian *rog*), it is often mistaken for the Russian *rozhok*. *Rozhok* is a conical instrument with a cup mouthpiece and five or six fingerholes. It is very difficult to play in tune and the mouthpiece is placed on the corner of the mouth. Whenever *rozhok* players live in neighbouring villages they meet to play together. Another type of Russian horn was made world-famous in the eighties of last century by N. Kondratyev's horn ensemble.

In the spring, when the Huculs drive their cattle out to pasture in the western Ukraine, the sounds of the *trembita*, made of white firwood, resounds from the mountain slopes. Its signals call the herds on rainy days when the mountains are hidden in thick fog. Typical among Russian idiophones is the *loshka* (spoon), usually a wooden or metal spoon with a long handle on which pellet bells are fixed. Two spoons are held between the fingers of the right hand and clashed together with their convex surfaces. Skilled musicians manage to use as many as four or five spoons. Sometimes one spoon is placed to the mouth which serves as a resonator, and by striking it with another spoon sounds of various pitch may be produced. In the Tula district the clapper *treshchotka* still occurs occasionally. It consists of about twenty wooden plaques threaded on a string and is played by women during wedding celebrations.

The accordion *harmonika (garmonika, garmon, garmoniya)*, which appeared in Russia soon after it was invented in the forties of last century, spread there with amazing speed and today is probably the most frequently used folk instrument. The efforts of the makers to adapt the accordion to the requirements of Russian folk music has given rise to many different types of construction. The *saratovskaya*, named after the town of Saratov where it was first made, belongs to the group of one row diatonic accordions. In contrast to the *livenskaya*, made at Livna, it produces different tones

Fragment of Russian folk song accompanied by the double flute *svirel*

when the bellows are expanded to those produced when compressed. Two-row accordions are more frequent. *Cherepoveckaya* was originally diatonic and, instead of three-note chords, had supplementary semi-tones in the bass. *Cherepachka*, as it was familiarly called, was produced in various sizes and the insufficient number of bass buttons was later eliminated by transferring the supplementary half-tones to the right-hand keyboard. Their place was taken by the bass buttons. This gave rise to the chromatic accordion *varshavska. Kasimovskaya* (after the town of Kasimov) has no ready three-note chords. Instead it has a rich bass permitting the formation of both

Russian market players. One of them is playing wooden spoons with rattles, called *loshki*

major as well as minor chords. The most perfect of all the Russian chromatic accordions is an instrument built at the turn of the century and named after the legendary Russian singer Bayan. *Bayan* usually possesses fifty-two keys placed on the right-hand keyboard in three rows with a compass of B-c⁴. The bass keyboard has one hundred buttons in five rows. The first and second row contains the basic and supplementary basses from G to f major, the third to fifth row produces major and minor three-note chords and the dominant seventh chords from any tone of the chromatic row. In the course of time various systems were developed and recently the *vyborniy bayan* has become most frequently used. After the Second World War the accordion, differing from the *bayan* only in the piano keyboard for the right hand, has become widely used.

Drawing after wall painting in the cathedral of Kiev, 11th century

Russian *harmonika* player

THE BALTIC STATES

LITHUANIA

The Lithuanians are convinced that their favourite national instrument *kankles* is of Lithuanian origin though it is well known that this instrument is equally popular among the neighbouring peoples. Originally the *kankles* had a wing-shaped corpus made of one piece; today it has a flat resonator box in the shape of a trapezoid made from lime, oak or alder wood. The top of the *kankles* slopes either from left to right or from right to left, which influences the manner of play and tuning. Metal strings in odd numbers (5, 7, 9 or more) are fixed to the tailpiece on the narrower side of the box and to the pegs on the wider side. The *kankles* is placed on the player's knees and the strings plucked (sometimes with a plectrum) by the fingers of the right hand while the left hand is used to dampen the strings. Skilled players use both hands for plucking the strings. In recent years a whole family of *kankles* has been built, each member with a special fitting for retuning the strings during play. On the contrabass *kankles* the strings are struck with a mallet.

A typical Lithuanian instrument is the flute-like *skuduchiay* related to the Russian *kuvikli*. It is used in ensembles of five or seven musicians, each of whom holds two or three whistles of differing length, which he puts to his lips alternately at the moment when his turn comes in the melody. The clarinet *birbine* is made from maple or ash wood. It has five to six fingerholes, a clarinet mouthpiece and a bell made from a cow's horn. The *toshiale* is a plaque of birch wood. It has a slightly bent corner which is placed to the lower lip. By blowing on the edge of the plaque a sharp penetrating sound is produced. If the *toshiale* is placed between the lower lip and the gums then the musician's hands are left free for playing the violin or accordion at the same time. The musician further makes use of his foot to strike the kettle-drum *kyalmas* fitted for this purpose with a pedal.

The Lithuanian *ozhgaris*, a horn with from three to five fingerholes, is identical to the Latvian *azharages* and the Estonian *sarvu*. *Ragas* is a shepherd's horn made from wood or an animal's horn. A set of wooden horns is made up of five instruments of differing length and tuned with the difference of one tone. In the ensemble the *ragas* is played similarly to the *skuduchiay*. The wooden trumpet *trimitas (daudites, triuba)* once used to be widely distributed among all Scandinavian peoples, but has survived only in Lithuania. *Skrabalas* is a set of wooden bells tuned diatonically and chromatically and fixed to a common frame. The bells are struck with wooden mallets.

Kokle, similar in shape and structure to the Lithuanian *kankles*, has become the symbol of Latvian folk music. The monochord *diga (dingas)*, with wooden rectangular corpus, once used to be an essential teaching aid used at schools for the teaching of music. The block flute *stabule* made of aspen, willow or pine wood once used to be a great favourite. Several variants existed differing from one another in the shape of the tube and the number of fingerholes. After the Second World War the *stabule* was revived, improved in construction and several different sizes of instrument created. The Latvian *taure* is made from the trunk of a young fir or pinetree. A larger variant of the *taure* with fingerholes is called *tashu taure*. Several idiophones are used in the State Ensemble of Folk Instruments. Similar to the Lithuanian *skrabalas* is the Latvian *koka zvans*, an instrument consisting of wooden cow-bells with a compass of $c^1—c^3$. Another two idiophones have been adapted to the needs of the State Ensemble of Folk Instruments, a clapper in the shape of a metal rod *trideksnis* and the pellet-bells *zvargulis*.

ESTONIA

As is the case of the other Baltic nations, the Estonians' favourite instrument is also a plucked chordophone, the *kannel*. A sort of chord-playing version of the *kannel, saate*

Latvian player with *birbine*

206

kannel, was widespread in the south of Estonia during the last century. It had major and minor strings placed in the manner of a keyboard, and the melody *kannel* with forty-seven strings in two rows, the upper corresponding to the white keys, and the lower, with red strings, to the black keys. The last type is the chord *kannel* with rectangular corpus and fourteen strings in courses of four tuned in major and minor thirds and fourths intervals. *Puyspill* is a bowed monochord whose scroll, neck and foot is formed from one long wooden rod with one gut string. An air-filled bladder is placed between the rod and string. *Mollpill*, another bowed monochord, consists of a long narrow resonance box with fingerboard and frets on the belly. The instrument is placed on a table and the string is shortened with the fingers of the left hand.

A whistle flute with three to eight fingerholes, named after the material from which it was made, is still to be found among shepherds. A whistle made from the twisted bark of a tree is *payupill*, from reed *soopill* and from metal *plekk-vilepill*. *Piibar (vene vile* = Russian whistle*)* is an interesting type actually representing two instruments with common head. The tube is made from bark peeled off the tree in one piece, with a lateral blowhole in the middle. Below and above are three fingerholes each. The instrument is held like a cross-flute and tones are produced in both parts of the tube. Since the length of the two parts of the tube is the same, and since the fingerholes are equidistant, both parts of the instrument produce the same tones. *Roopill*, a thin bamboo reed with five or six fingerholes, resembles the *ruska zhaleyka*. The bagpipes *torupill*, with one chanter and two drone pipes and the bag made from a cow's stomach, is much in use. *Yachi-plibar (yachi-pazun)*, a metal horn covered with skin, has survived in the south of Estonia. From among the idiophones the scraper *kraatespill* has survived, a wooden stick struck on or scraped over the floor when a dance has reached its climax. During the Second World War two variants of

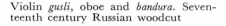

Violin *gusli*, oboe and *bandura*. Seventeenth century Russian woodcut

the *kraatespill* were made. One consists of a stick with a bent, thickened lower end, while the other has the shape of a narrow wooden rectangular beam with two oval indentations over which metal strings have been stretched. When they are struck they produce a sound similar to the scratching of a hard broom when the floor is swept.

The historical contacts between the musical cultures of the various nations of the Soviet Union were favourable influence in the development of folk creation. Forms of reproduction have also changed quickly and the armoury of instruments is constantly being revised. Above all work on the reconstruction and improvement of old folk instruments has become the basic creative programme of many research institutes (cf. Petrosyans and Didenko in Uzbekistan). However, apart from ensembles using only reconstructed and improved musical instruments, there exist many that play only on original instruments. The excellent results achieved in the music folklore of the nations of the Soviet Union is also due to the 'Decades of National Art' regularly held in Moscow and the music schools where folk instruments are taught and musicians, conductors and teachers of folk music creation are being trained.

185. Tuvinian woman with bowed *pyzanchi*

186. Tuvinian instrumental ensemble

187

188

187. Buryat violin *khuuchir* and flute *limba*

188. Tuvinian woman singing to the accompaniment of the *pyzanchi*

189. Kazakh bowed instrument *kobyz*

190. Kachinz zither *chatchan* (*chat'han*)

189

190

191

192

191. *Dutar* from Kazakhstan

192. Azerbaijan musicians
with *dutar*

193

194

193. Instrument maker's workshop in Dushanbe, the capital of Tadzhikistan

194. Kazakh musical instruments

195

196

197

198

195. Uzbek singer with *tar*

196. Daghestan musicians with drums *baraban*

197. South Ossetian woman with *dutar*

198. Performance on the *shuvyr*, the bagpipe of the Mari

199

199. Uzbek trumpet *karnaj* and tambourine *dojra*

200. Turkmenian folk musicians

201. Uzbek fiddle *kemanje*

202. Kirghiz chordophone *kiyak*

200

201

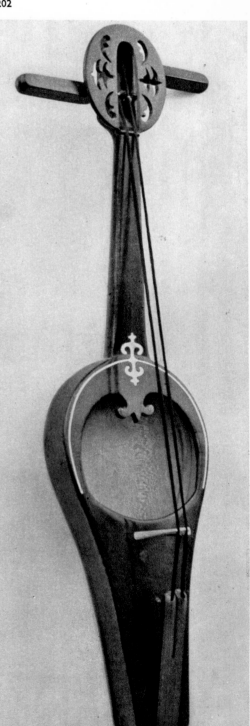

202

203

203. Kirghiz tambourine *dojra*

204. Uzbek shawm *surnaj*

205. Uzbek dulcimer *chang*

206. Ensemble of Uzbek folk musicians

204

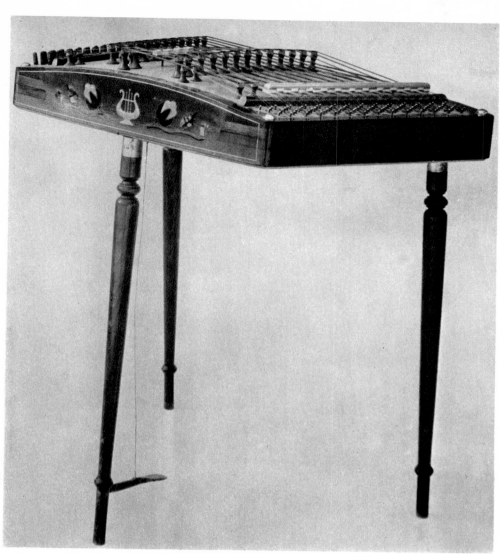

205

207

208

207. Uzbek *rubab*

208. Kazakh women playing *domra*

209. Mari *gusle*

210. Ensemble of Russian *gusle* players

211

212

213

214

211. Ensemble of Russian *harmonika* players

212. Ensemble of Tyrolese wind instruments from the Tarnopol region

213. Estonian boy with shepherd's trumpet

214. Transcarpathian *sopilkas*

215. Ukrainian *bandura* players

216. Byelorussian women with dulcimers

EUROPE

Instrumental folk music in Europe is so far the least investigated sphere of musical creation. Whereas among the non-European nations instrumental music forms the basis of musical culture, determining to a considerable degree the character of interpretation, scales, and rhythm in the sphere of the folk song, the folk music of the European nations has been arrested in its growth. Under the influence of classical music secondary folklore music was created, influenced by autochthonous folk music but transcribed and adjusted in various ways. These formations submit a distorted picture of instrumental folk music devoid of its artistic foundation, its vital expressiveness of content. And this is why original instrumental folk music can only rarely be found in Europe.

If we want to submit a survey of the European peoples' folk instruments, we must divide the continent into larger geographical units, even though I am fully aware of the dangers of such a division. For no nation in Europe could prevent reciprocal penetration of folk music and instruments, especially in neighbouring regions, since frontiers set by political formations, and not ethnics, are only very rarely the correct frontiers of musical folklore.

NORTHERN EUROPE

All the men that were there
stood up and uncovered their heads.
And however many women there were there,
all covered their faces in their hands,
the maidens' eyes were full of tears,
the young men knelt.
All the animals from the forest
hid their claws and lay down
to listen to the kantele
and, when they had listened, they were
enchanted.
From the neck of beechwood,
there come sounds of love and pride;
the fingerboard is of ebony,
and therefore you sing so sweet and pure —
and with your taut wire strings
you break all the hearts in the land . . .

Kalevala (rune 44) the rise of the kantele

Folk music of the peoples of Northern Europe in comparison with other regions seems to be comparatively the most effective and sober. Voices are duller, interpretation more monotonous. And it is probably this sobriety of musical performance that has brought the chordophone to the fore in Scandinavia. The task of the string instrument is above all to accompany dancing, whereas plucked instruments are used more as solo instruments or to accompany vocal music. Since Scandinavia possesses highly developed cattle-breeding, it has a considerable number of horn and whistle aerophones. Membranophones are less frequent and limited to cylindrical drums with two heads. The number of idiophones is negligible. Similarly, as in other parts of Europe, the accordion is gaining in popularity in the North.

FINLAND

Since time immemorial Finnish folk singers have sung their rune songs to the accompaniment of the *kantele*. According to legend the first *kantele* was made by one of the heroes in the Kalevala from the skull of a huge pike. The resonator of the *kantele* is made of alder, pine or birch wood and is wing-shaped. The number of strings has increased in the course of time from the original five, tuned g¹, a¹ b flat¹, c², d², to thirty. At the end of the last century the *kantele* almost disappeared in Finland, but now it is again very much in vogue. *Jouhikko (jouhikantele)* is thought to have reached Finland via Sweden from the Celtic cultural region. Related to the Estonian *hijukannel*, it has a strongly convex back and a flat belly. There is a handhole on the left instead of the fingerboard, through which the musician pushes his fingertips to stop the strings. During play the instruments are placed on the left leg, with its lower end resting against the right knee. The three-string *versikannel* is of the same construction as the Latvian *diga* and the Estonian *mollpill*. Shepherd's instruments include the reed *lira* and *ludda*, as well as the wooden trumpets *tjurja* and *torvi*.

Fragment of a melody from the Kalevala

One of the most ancient folk instruments of Sweden, *strakharpa* is related to the Finnish *jouhikko*. In shape it resembles the medieval *crwth* of ancient Wales, the Icelandic fiddle and the Estonian *talharpa*. An interesting remnant of the past is also the *nyckelharpa (nyckelfiol)*, with Sweden as the only country in which it has survived.

SWEDEN

NORWAY

Swedish *strakharpa*

There is evidence that the *nyckelharpa* once existed in Germany under the name *Schlüssel-fiedel*. In the Danish countryside it was called *nöglefelein* and in Norway *lökkelje*. The *nyckelharpa* developed from the medieval *fidula* to which the tangent mechanism of the hurdy-gurdy was applied to stop the strings. This is why the *nyckelharpa* lacks the little wheel to sound the strings; a bow is used instead. The older types possess only one row of tangents and are called *kontrabasharpa*. *Silverbasharpa*, a more recent instrument, has four of five melody strings tuned a¹, c¹ g, c, and a varying number of drone strings. The Swedish *hummel* is closely related to the Norwegian zither *langeleik*, the Danish *humel* and the Dutch *hommel*. It is usually of rectangular shape with metal frets on the left edge. The drone strings are tuned to tonic and dominant. In the 1830's Johann Dillner, a priest from Osterval, invented a bowed zither *psalmodikon (notstocken)*, which was played at church, and at schools was a useful aid in teaching singing. The *psalmodikon* first had a rectangular corpus. In the course of time it assumed a cello shape with frets, one melody and four to eight drone strings.

Records have been preserved of minstrel singers in Norway who played the *fele (fedil, hardangerfelen)*. According to tradition the *fele* was invented in the seventeenth century by a teacher from Ostersje, Lars Klark, and later improved to its present condition by his pupil Isak Nielsen Botnen. Botnen's son Thrond became famous as the builder of the Hardanger *fele*. In 1850 the great Norwegian violinist Ole Bull gave a concert in Bergen together with one of the most talented minstrel musicians (who was known throughout the country by the nickname Möllergutten, and whose real name was Thorgeir Adundson Ødegaarden) playing the *fele*. The Hardanger *fele* has replaced most of the other folk instruments in Norway and may therefore be justly called the Norwegian national instrument. The oldest Norwegian chordophone is *langeleik*, a type of psaltery with a variety of shapes, mostly wing-shaped or rectangular, with four to fourteen diatonically tuned metal strings. From the wind instruments the long shepherd's horn *lur*, made of wood or birch bark, and the small horn *prillar*, made of an ox or goat horn on which long-drawn-out songs and folk dances are accompanied, have survived.

CENTRAL EUROPE

Historical events in Central Europe resulted in some ethnical groups living in comparative isolation whereas others for a longer period of time were exposed to the strong influence of western civilization. Different geographical, social, religious and economic conditions led also to considerable differentiation. In contrast to the northern, and, to some extent, eastern peoples, Central Europe has relatively more idiophones: scrapers, rattles, clappers, leaf and grass reeds, bells, etc. Great typological variation is achieved by the bowed chordophones. Plucked instruments are the main feature of eastern Europe, whereas struck chordophones (dulcimer) belong mainly to Central Europe. Flutelike instruments and instruments with mouthpieces prevail among the aerophones; less well represented are reed instruments, with the exception of some kinds made by shepherds or children from twisted bark. On the other hand, there are many types of bagpipes and in recent years the harmonika and accordion have penetrated the band of traditional folk instruments.

Polish folk musicians. Left to right: fiddle, bagpipe and flute. Eighteenth century woodcut

POLAND   Poland is the land of bagpipes. Young herdsmen, to while away the time, prepare to become bagpipe players by practising on a pipe with bladder similar to the medieval *platerspiel*. It is called *siesienki*, has a cylindrical tube with six fingerholes (the seventh is a rear thumbhole) and upturned bell. The reed is vibrated by the compressed air in the bladder which is blown up through a short mouthpiece. The Polish bagpipes have a bag of goatskin into which the player drives air by means of a small bellows held under the right arm. The left arm presses on the air-filled bag driving the air into two reeds, one melody and one drone. Both reeds terminate in a cow's horn and beaten brass bell. *Koziol* is another type of bagpipe, somewhat larger and with longer pipes. The bag is made of a whole kidskin with the fur and the chanter pipe decorated with a carved kid's head and not a goat's head, as is the case in ordinary bagpipes. *Koziol slubny* (wedding bagpipe) used to be a ritual instrument for wedding celebrations, played, however, only up to the wedding dinner, when the piper exchanged them for the big *koziol*.

Mazanki (from the word *mazani* = drawing the bow over the strings) played together with the *koziol slubny* is a small violin with three strings tuned in fourths, but a fifth higher than the ordinary violin. *Mazanki* is made of one piece, with pinewood top and bridge (the right foot of which passes through a soundhole into the corpus and rests on its back). In the Shamotul region an ancient folk instrument has been preserved resembling today's contrabass, with the upper part of the corpus of angular shape. Once, however, the *maryna*, as the instrument is called in Poland to this day, consisted of a long spike that passed through the rectangular box-shaped pinewood resonator narrowing towards the top. At the top the spike formed the neck with scroll and pegs, surmounted by metal rings or brass saucers that rattled when the *maryna* was tapped against the floor during performance. Two or three gut strings are tuned in fifths, G-d or A-e.

From among wind instruments Polish folk instruments include flutes without fingerholes, of which *fujarka wielkopostna* is identical to the Slovak *koncovka* (endblown flute). *Fujara salasznikowa* (shepherd's *fujara*) is nearly two metres long and therefore

Polish musicians

its bottom opening is closed by means of a valve worked by a lever. The long *trabita* is identical to the Ukrainian *trembita* and the Slovak *fujara trombita*. *Rog pastierski* (shepherd's horn) is very rare, occurring only in the southern mountain regions of Poland. In the Lubsko region various whistles, clappers and rattles have been preserved, used by children as acoustic toys.

In those parts of Czechoslovakia where the population is concerned with cattle breeding, a certain type of instrumental music has developed from signals used to call the herds and to send news from the pastures down to the village, and from the intimate musical performance of the shepherds, which is unique in Central Europe as far as its authentic character in Slovakia is concerned. Throughout almost the whole of Slovakia the block flute *pastierska pishtala* (shepherd's flute) is to be found, with six fingerholes and made from various types of wood, the tube either turned or carved. A special feature of playing is the treble-touch whereby the musician excludes three fingerholes, using only the remaining three. By overblowing he manages to produce the entire chromatic scale. Treble-touch is used with normal playing technique thus obtaining a compass up to two and a half octaves. *Rifova pishtala (koncovka)* made from young hazelnut shoots is an end-blown flute without fingerholes. By covering the endhole of the tube with the index finger of the left hand two rows of partial tones may be produced, of which the most frequently used are the third to seventh or seventh to thirteenth partial tone. *Dvojachka* is a double flute with two pipes of equal length. One has fingerholes, and the other is a drone pipe.

An instrument holding a unique position among European folk instruments, not only as far as construction but also as far as instrumental music is concerned, is the *fujara*. It is the instrument of alpine shepherds, played on the pastures high up in the mountains. The *fujara* is a type of bass end-blown flute about 140 to 200 cm long. Parallel with the longitudinal axis another, narrower tube with short mouthpiece is fixed with the aid of a leather strap or brass wire to the upper, closed end of the tube. There are three fingerholes in the lower part of the main tube, at a considerable distance from each other. Of the compass of about three octaves only about one half can be used, since the deepest tones are too low and the highest not pure in intonation. A characteristic musical effect on the *fujara* is the 'rozfuk', a signal by which the musician warms up at the beginning of the play. He plays all tones in a compass of two octaves to demonstrate as well as possible the particular acoustic properties of the instrument. First a nasal sound is heard, then the melody descends gradually from the high tone forming small motifs, through playful ornamental figures to the basic tone. A characteristic tone series on the *fujara* is mixolydian and hypoionic: d, e, f sharp, g, a, b, c¹, d¹, which tonally and from the point of view of interpretation has strongly influenced the creation of the characteristic Slovak folk songs.

During the warm summer evenings, when shadows grow longer and the first twilight extends over the pasture, the long-drawn-out tones of *bachovska trouba (fujara trombita)* may be heard, by which the shepherd calls the geldings to drive home the sheep. It is identical to the Czech *pastyrska trouba*, also called *valashska* or *salashska trouba*. In Slovakia the *bachovska trouba* reaches a length of five to five and a half metres. The slightly conical wooden tube, wrapped round with cherry or birch bark, rests on a raised point or on the shoulder of the musician's assistant. A variation of the *fujara trombita* is *vazhecky roh*, which is shorter and always turned up, since it is made from the root of a fir. The Slovak bagpipes *gajdy* are made from lamb or kidskin turned inside out. The chanter pipe with five to six fingerholes and the long drone pipe are adorned with metal incrustations. The head of the chanter pipe is adorned with stylized figural carvings. Both pipes terminate in a bell made from an ox horn and brass.

Chordophones are represented by the violin, viola, violoncello, contrabass, and only one folk variant of the violin *zhlobcovky*, which has a slightly piriform corpus made of one piece. Influenced by gypsy music the dulcimer spread throughout Slovakia. The Jew's harp *drumbla* has now become an instrument of the past. The same holds good for two idiophones, the rattle *rapkach* and the clapper *klepach*. *Bunkosh* is a stick with brass rings used for dances. A variation of the *bunkosh* is *zhdiarska valashka*. The shepherd's stick *kulagha* with jingles on the handle is a similar instrument.

Czech wedding song for two violins and bagpipe

Czech bagpiper

231

Signals played by Slovak shepherd's trumpet

Slovak shepherd with *fujara*

Hungarian folk melody for the shepherd's flute *furulya*

The only folk instrument to have survived in Bohemia up to the present is the *dudy* (bagpipes). Though all the types of this widespread European folk instrument show certain similarities, each cultural region has its own differences in construction, acoustics, and above all in performance. This also holds good for the Czech bagpipes which consist of a melody pipe with seven fingerholes, and a drone pipe, a bag made from the skin of a year-old goat into which air is driven by bellows placed under the player's left arm. The drone pipe produces E flat, the melody pipe b flat, d^1, e flat^1, f, g^1, a flat^1, b flat^1, c^2. Since the pipe lacks the upper seventh (d^2), this tone does not usually occur in tunes for the bagpipe. The pipers try to overcome the fact that their play is always in the same scale by joining in the play of other instruments, embellishing them with variation and intermezzos.

The first records concerning Hungarian folk musicians, 'igric' and 'regösh' date from the tenth century. The term 'igric' (player) points to old contacts between Hungarian folk music and Slavonic culture. Among Hungarian folk instruments there are hardly any (except the Jew's harp *szájdoromb*) that the Hungarians definitely brought with them from their Asian homeland. The most common shepherd's block flute *furulya* is identical in construction and appearance to the Slovak shepherd's whistle. The *tilinko* is related to the Rumanian wooden whistle *tilinca ca dup*. It still occurs among the Hungarian minority in Rumania. The Hungarian bagpipes *duda* have a joint chanter and drone pipe made from one piece of wood. *Kanásztülök* is a cow's horn used to drive the cattle to pasture. The influence of the neighbouring peoples is evident also in the *citera* with its rectangular resonator, two fingerboard strings and eight accompanying open strings. *Forgólant (tekerö, nyenyere)* is a four-stringed hurdy-gurdy tuned to A, a, d^1, e^1. The second string is raised by a wooden block which, when turning the wheel steeped in rosin, produces a cracking sound and thus a special rhythmical stress.

The national instrument of Hungary is the dulcimer *cimbalom* used in the folk music of many European nations. Half the strings are divided with the aid of two bridges at a ratio of 2:3 so that the divided strings are tuned in fifths. To attain two different sound effects the mallets on one end are covered with felt, and on the other side they are left bare. The modern Hungarian *pedálcimbalom* (pedal dulcimer) resting on four legs was designed by the instrument maker J. Schunda of Budapest in 1874. It has a damper pedal; some of its strings are not divided at all, some are divided twice with the aid of one bridge and some even three times with the aid of two bridges. The lowest register, from D-B, is trichord, the central from c-f runs in courses of four and the high from f-e^3 in courses of five. The aerophone *tarogato*, with wide conical tube, clarinet mouthpiece and modern key mechanism is also regarded as a national instrument.

Rumanian folk musicians — 'lautari' — are called after the instrument on which they accompany their songs and which was named, apparently under Turkish influence, *kobza*. The *kobza* is lute-shaped with an almond-shaped corpus glued together from wide strips of maple wood. The belly of pine has several sound slits. The upper part of the corpus narrows and suddenly changes into a short neck with pegbox turned back at an angle. Of the four metal strings tuned to fourths (dd^1, aa^1, dd, gg^{1}g^1), the first three are bichord strings, the fourth trichord. They are placed

Slovak shepherd's trumpet

232

in an order opposite to that which is normal for string instruments, i.e. the lowest strings are on the right of the instrument. The *kobza* was mainly an accompanying instrument whose place has been taken by the dulcimer *tambal*, which has spread quickly among folk musicians.

The *nai* (from the Arabic), in the form in which it is being played today in Rumania, has many related forms inside and outside Europe, for it is a pan-pipe particularly widespread in Moldavia and Muntenia. It consists of eight to twenty-four wooden pipes of varying length and bore diameter, stopped at the end and arranged in raft form. The manner of producing tones and of playing is the same for *nai* as for any other pan-pipes. The musician passes the instrument quickly in front of his lips, thus producing a bubbling, clear trill. Shepherds' music and instruments made by the shepherds hold an important place in Rumanian folk music. Favourites up to the present day are the block flute without fingerholes *tilinca ca dup* (with fipple) identical to the Ukrainian *telenka* and the Hungarian *tilinko*, and its more primitive colleague, the open flute *tilinca far dup* (without fipple), made from reed and strengthened at some points by cherry bark or string wound round it. One of the many folk songs tells of the shepherd that lost his flute *fluier*. To make himself a new instrument he stole a shaft and for this he was brought before the judge by the village people. But when the judge heard the shepherd play he was so charmed that he let him go free. The *fluier* is made of wood and has six fingerholes. The bagpipe *cimpoi* has a bag of goatskin. The openings left from the hindlegs are sewn up, and the opening of the neck and the front legs are made airtight with plugs. In these a chanter and a drone pipe are inserted. It is for work rather than pleasure that the long wooden horn *bucium (tulnic)* is used by Rumanian shepherds. Its name reminds one of the ancient Roman *buccina*. Signals are produced on it with the aid of partial tones, the number of which depends not only on the instrument's construction but also on the musician's skill.

Melody for the Rumanian shepherd's flute *tilinca* from Bela Bartok's collection

Rumanian musician playing pan-pipe *nai*

Every region of Bulgaria has its musical instruments, mainly of Persian-Arabic origin that reached Bulgaria via Turkey. The *tambura*, typical of south-west Bulgaria, is a four-string plucked instrument with a strongly convex corpus and long neck with metal frets. The *gadulka*, a bowed instrument, is popular in western Bulgaria, as well as the double flute *dvojanka* and the bagpipe *gajda* with chanter and drone

Instrumental introduction to a Bulgarian folk song

pipe. Thrace is richest in folk instruments: apart from the *gadulka* and *gajda* the shepherd's flute *tristavnijat kaval* is also played, technically a very varied instrument, on which a skilful musician can give an amazing performance. He can fully use the range of three octaves on one breath. A reed is sometimes fitted into the head of the *kaval*, which is then called *kaval kudop*. *Gadulka (gusle)* is a bowed instrument with piriform corpus suddenly changing into a short neck without fingerboard that terminates in a flat scroll. The belly of pine has two semi-circular soundholes and a bridge resting on it with its shorter leg, the longer passing through the soundhole and resting on the back of the instrument. When played the *gadulka* rests on the knee in a vertical position and the nails of the left hand lightly touch the strings, producing flageolet tones. The big Bulgarian drum *tupan (topan)* with wooden corpus and laced membranes is identical to the drum of the same name to be found in Albania, Macedonia and southern Serbia. It is struck with a short wooden mallet with a round head.

SOUTH-EAST
AND SOUTHERN EUROPE

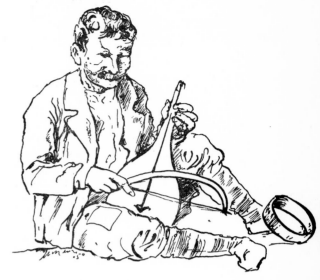

Serbian *guslar*

The folk music of south-east and southern Europe does not greatly differ from the music of the other European regions. It is just possible that in some countries (mainly in Italy), it is more closely connected with church rituals (*pifferari* in Italy). On the whole it is the diatonic music and chromatism in the most easterly regions that must be ascribed to the Arabic-Turkish influence. The armoury of instruments showing signs of the cultures of all previous rulers of the Mediterranean region is very colourful. Some types of drums betray their Arabic origin in their names; idiophones are represented by various clapped and scraped xylophones and metallophones. Among wind instruments reed clarinets are most frequent. It seems that they express best the features most typical of Mediterranean instrumental music.

YUGOSLAVIA

In Montenegro the most important expression of folk music to this day has remained an epic song of a recitative character accompanied by the most typical chordophone of Yugoslavia, *gusle*. In Serbia this instrument has survived only in the western mountain regions. It is of Asian origin and was known among the Slavs as early as at the time of Byzantium. The corpus of the *gusle* is made of one block, the belly covered with sheep, ass or rabbit skin. The short neck with big peg terminates in a stylized scroll. One horsehair string is fixed to the peg and is stretched over a high bridge. Three shapes of the *gusle* corpus may be distinguished, the Serbian which is trapezoid, the Bosnian which is hexagonal and the Montenegrin which is piriform. The bow has preserved its archaic arched shape with straight handle. The manner of production, the material used and the decorations indicate the ancient pastoral culture. The instrument is held on the knee or placed between the knees. During play the strings are stopped by a sideways pressure of the fingers. A sliding movement of the fingers produces a glissando.

Shepherds' calls 'Ojkanje' with *gusle* accompaniment in the special notation of G. Becking

SERBS

The main part of folk music in Serbia is made up by *gusle* melodies, though at the present time the *gusle* has been replaced in many parts of the region by more modern instruments, especially the *tambura (ichiterliji)* and the accordion. The *tamburina* once used to have an ovoid corpus and long neck; this has been changed for an almond-shaped corpus with a wider and shorter neck, metal frets and a head with screw mechanism. The most popular wind instruments are still the double flute, made of one piece of wood with two mouthpieces, and pipes (one with three, the other with four fingerholes), the *kaval* and *shupeljka*, which are variants of the block flute with six fingerholes, and the bagpipes *diple* and *dude*.

CROATS

In Croatia a current folk instrument is the double clarinet *diple*. If it has an air reservoir it is called *mih (mishnice)*. *Vele sopele* (big *sopele*) and *male sopele* (small *sopele*) are instruments with double reeds, always played together. *Jedinka* is a single block flute different from *dvojka*, a double flute. *Lirica* is the oldest type of Mediterranean instrument found on the Dalmatian coast. Three strings are tuned to first, large second and fifth.

SLOVENES

Among the Slovenes folk instruments play a less important part than among the other peoples of Yugoslavia. In the villages instruments other than folk instruments are played today. Some flute-like instruments such as *pishchal*, *fuchkec*, *trobec* and *zhvegla* are still preserved. *Costimaje* is a pan-pipe with six reed pipes of varying length bound together in threes between two small wooden boards. Up till recently the friction drum *gudalo* or *muga* served as bass accompaniment to round dances 'kolo'. Formerly the Jew's harp *drumelca (brumbice)* used to be played more, as well as the dulcimer *oprekelj (shenterija)*.

MACEDONIA	The musical tradition of Macedonia bears traces of Byzantine culture and Turkish rule. Both wind instruments, the flute *kaval* and shawm *zurla (zurna)* are of Turkish origin. *Duduk, shupelka, svirol* and *dvojanka* are of Slavonic origin, however. Some membranophones such as the big drum *tupan* and the goblet drum *tarabuka* recall Turkish rule.
ALBANIA	The main instruments of Albania are the shawm *zurla*, the bagpipe *roga* and the big drum *tupan*. In the tonal series produced on the *roga* whole and semi-tones alternate regularly. This tonal series that belongs neither to the old church modes nor to the European Major-Minor system, shows marked similarity to the east Turkish tonal series. Play on the *tupan* calls forth equal amazement, since the beats are irregular and do not agree with the accent of the melody they accompany.
GREECE	Efforts to preserve the tradition of folk music in Greece have made it possible to use various types of folk instruments which, together with vocal music, create a colourful heterophony influenced by the east. On Lady Day and St Lazarus, Epirian shepherds accompany their song with the bells *kudhunia* that are normally put round the neck of cattle. They hold them in their hands or fix them to their elbows. Tong-shaped metal clappers *massa* are a Greek speciality, serving in Thrace as rhythmical accompaniment to song on the 'calends' (the first days of the months). The Turkish influence on the Greek armoury of musical instruments is shown in the number of membranophones of which the double membrane drum *dauli* is used in continental Greece to accompany melodic instruments, above all the shawm *zurna*. *Dauli* in Macedonia may attain a diameter of up to one metre; on the islands it is smaller and is called *tumbi (tumbaneli)*. The musician sits, holding the drum between his legs and striking it either with two mallets or with his hands. The tambourine *defi* or *daires* is found in the continental regions. On Cyprus it is larger and called *tambucha*. In the north and on some islands the clay goblet drum *tumbeleki* or *tarabuka* is played.

Bagpipes are played to the accompaniment of drums. In Greece two varieties are to be found. On the islands they are called *tsambuna (ascomadura, tsambunofilaca, ascavli, tulumi,* etc.) and possess a sheepskin bag with short double reed and horn bell. In the north the *gaida* is played; this possesses a chanter as well as a drone pipe. Throughout continental Greece shepherds play the cross flute *floyer* with six or seven fingerholes. The end-blown block flute *suravli* and *floyer* are often replaced on Crete by the clarinet called *madura*. This is a short reed pipe with idioglot of thin sheet metal. Shawm instruments are represented by the *zurna (caramuza, pipiza, niacaro)* from the instruments of Oriental nations. They are always played to the accompaniment of the drum *dauli* and such a duo is called *zighia*, in contrast to the modern ensemble *compania* made up of violin, clarinet, lute and dulcimer.

Plucked chordophones of the lute family have been preserved as folk instruments. The lute with short neck is called *uti*. Four double strings and one chanterelle are tuned in fourths, with the exception of the first low string which forms an interval of a large second with the following string. *Uti* is being gradually replaced by the lute *laghuto (xilo)* which has a longer neck and metal frets. Four double strings are tuned in fifths C, G, d, a. *Sazi, baglamas, buzuki* and many other plucked instruments, named differently in various regions, such as *yongari, tamburas, kiteli, hurgari,* etc., correspond with their Oriental counterparts in shape and construction. *Canonaki* is identical to the Arabic *kanun*, and *sanduri* is a dulcimer with chromatically tuned strings and a compass of from three to four octaves.

Bowed instruments are represented by fiddles of varying types that may be roughly divided into two groups. The first contains piriform fiddles used on the islands and in the northern part of continental Greece, the other consists of Caucasian fiddles with narrow elongated corpus used on the Pontus. Most fiddles have three strings tuned in fifths g, d¹, a¹. The fiddle of the Dodecanese has a central drone string and is tuned c¹, g, d¹ or also four strings tuned in the 'Turkish manner' G, d, a, d¹. *Kemanes*, the fiddle of Capadocia, has six strings tuned to fifths and fourths and the same number of drone strings. The musician sits holding the fiddle on his left knee, either perpendicularly or slightly inclined. If he stands he rests the fiddle against his waist. The instrument is played with a bow on which pellet-bells *yeracocudhuna* have been fixed and the strings are also touched with the fingers in flageolet technique.

Thracian youth with clapper *massa*

Somewhere there is a herd grazing in the mountains of Abruzzi in Italy. And somewhere from the distance the quiet sound of the shawm may be heard. A shepherd is playing a melody that his father and grandfather have played before him. Similar tunes sound from the slope opposite and an old shepherd with a pipe slowly descends from the heights. It is Christmas, and people are celebrating the birth of Christ. The shepherds are descending to the valleys to announce the joyful news. They are going to Rome, the Eternal City, full of churches and painted Madonnas. Before them stand the *pifferari* (from *piva* = bagpipe or *piffero* = shawm; *pifferaro* = piper) with their pipes, shawms or oboes, and round them a crowd of children and adults. The greatest number of whistle instruments has been preserved in Sicily. Often they are decorated with pictures of patron saints. A special instrument is formed by a terracotta vessel held by the handle. A kind of droning sound is produced by blowing into the neck. A similar sound is produced in Naples by the friction drum *caccavella* (*cupa-cupa* in Apulia). The most typical instrument, however, is the *launeddas* of the Abruzzi shepherds. It consists of three reed pipes of varying length. The shorter has five square fingerholes. The longer is a drone pipe and can be extended by prolonging the tube. The idioglot beating reed cut into the small mouthpiece is shaped like a swallow's tail. The third tube is the shortest, not connected with the other two, but free and has five to six fingerholes. An ensemble made up of *launeddas* is called *cunzertu launeddas* and plays during folk celebrations, and in front of the church during church and wedding processions.

Tricballac (tricca-balacca) is an instrument made of three mallets, the handles of which join to form a kind of fan. The frame rests firmly on the central mallet which is fixed and the outer ones, to which metal plaques are fixed, are free to strike against it. The scraper *vajasse (sveglia ragazze)* is formed by two sticks, one smooth and the other dentated. One end of the smooth stick is held below the musician's chin like a violin, the other end is held by the left hand. The other dentated stick to which sheet-metal plaques are fixed is passed over the smooth stick and produces a scratching rattling sound. Wooden idiophones include the castanets *nacchere* of Naples, two disc-shaped wooden boards. The *colascione*, a long lute, is a descendant of the Persian-Arabic *tanbura*.

WESTERN EUROPE

Catalonian boy with Jew's harp *verimbao*

In contrast to the other regions of Europe where aerophones and drums prevail, western Europe is dominated by bowed chordophones. Folklore has here been almost completely extinguished by the development of modern technology, industrialization and urbanization. In the Germanic countries traditional instrumental folk music was changed by the Reformation in the sixteenth century, the introduction of choral singing and the harmony and rhythm of classical music, to such a degree that only some slight traces of original folk music have been preserved in south Germany. Here and there some traditional customs appear on the most important Church holidays which are still accompanied by some simple instruments. This includes, for example, the ratchet, in German *Ratsche*, in French *crécelle*, in Italian *raganella* and in Spanish *carraca*. The Christian Church replaced the ritual of the winter solstice by St Martin's Day. Between Christmas and Twelfth Night boys in Flanders walk from house to house playing the friction drum *rommelpot*. This consists of an ordinary earthenware pot closed at the top by a membrane. A bundle of horsehair penetrates the centre of the bladder and is fixed to the bottom of the pot. Quite often *rommelpot* is made from flowerpots or bladders.

In central France the *vielle à roue*, regarded as a typical European instrument, has been preserved. Among some nations of Central Europe it has a flat corpus, but in France it is ovoid. The view that efforts to mechanize playing technique played an important part in the rise of the *vielle à roue* is without foundation. The inventors were concerned only with producing a string instrument that would produce not only the melody but at the same time a harmonic accompaniment. For this purpose a wooden wheel covered with leather and varnished with resin was used, turned with the aid of a handle, and a keyboard mechanism with a small number of tangents. The wheel guarantees continuous sound, and the keys permit playing in several voice simultaneously.

Apart from the sharply defined chordophones, there exist instruments made from plant material, reeds from grasses, whistles from bark, etc. It is usually children that make these instruments. In Germany a friction instrument, *Waldteufel*, is sold in the Christmas markets, known in Flanders as *ronker*, in Coventry, England, as *hoo'r*, in France as *bourdon* and in Gascogne as *arran*. This consists of a pasteboard or tin cylinder closed at one end by parchment. A string is passed through the membrane and tied to the notched handle of a stick by which it is rotated, producing a humming noise. Another instrument is a heritage of the past, already frequently mentioned in connection with non-European instruments. This is the *Jew's harp*, in German *Maultrommel*, in French *guimbarde*, and in Spanish *verimbao*. It used to be widespread throughout Europe. Today it occurs only in two regions situated a very great distance from each other, in Rumania and in Spain.

In the west there are only a few shawms, played in lower Brittany, together with bagpipes *(bombarde)*. Bagpipes that used to be very popular in Flanders, as may be seen from Brueghel's pictures, have now disappeared from the area. On the other hand, in some countries they have become a national instrument. In Ireland two types may be found: *piob mor* is identical to the Scottish *Highland pipe* and *piob uillean* with the English *union pipe*. Even more important in Ireland is the harp that was represented originally by rectangular and triangular instruments. From the small triangular harp of Nordic origin that used to be worn at the waist in the Middle Ages, the simple diatonic *Irish harp* has developed. This instrument requires a considerable amount of skill since each string is damped immediately after sounding, before the

Friction drum *Waldteufel*

IRISH HARP

next string is played. The *Irish harp* used to be played with long nails and not the fingertips, the right hand playing bass and the left descant, the melody often accompanied in octaves.

Alboka is an archaic shepherd's instrument that has survived among the Basques of Spain. Two bamboo or wooden pipes are tied together and cradled in a wooden gutter. One pipe has five, the other three, fingerholes producing tones tuned to a^1, c^2, d^2, e^2, f sharp^2. The idioglot beating reeds are protected by a horn mouth bell. The lower end terminates in a common cow-horn bell. Equally popular among the Basques is the tabor pipe *txistu*. The musician plays it with the left hand and beats the *tamboril* with the right. These two instruments form an important component of the Cobla folk dance ensemble from the vicinity of Barcelona. There still exist some folk instruments in Portugal whose names indicate their Arabic origin. They include the lute *alaud*, the square tambourine *aduf* and the primitive bowed chordophone *rebecca*.

As elsewhere in the world, the last remnants of traditional folk instruments in western Europe are being replaced by the accordion. It has become the national instrument of the French. In England it is hexagonal and called concertina. The Basques like the *trikitixa (sonue)* which in the construction of tone series has been fully adapted to the requirements of Basque folk music. It is usually played to accompany a singer using the tambourine *panderoyotzale*.

ALBOKA

Basque musician playing pipe and tabor

Polish folk musicians with trumpets

217. Norwegian zither *langeleik*

218. Norwegian violin *hardangerfele*

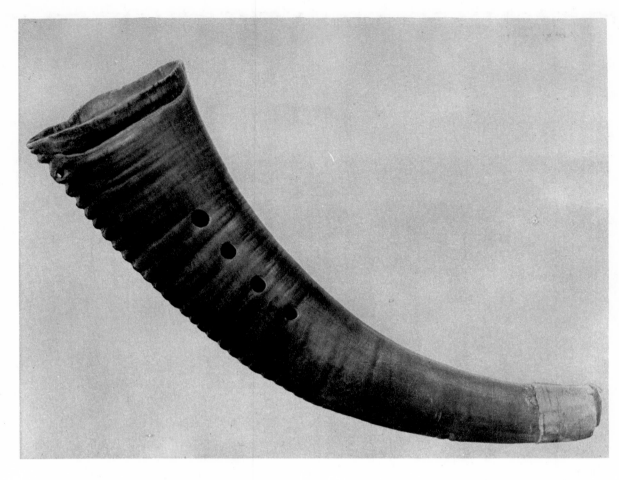

219

220

219. Finnish horn *paimensarvi*

220. Finnish *kantele*

222

221. Finnish peasant-woman playing the *kantele*

222.—224. Norwegian violin *hardangerfele* with case

223 **224**

225

226

227

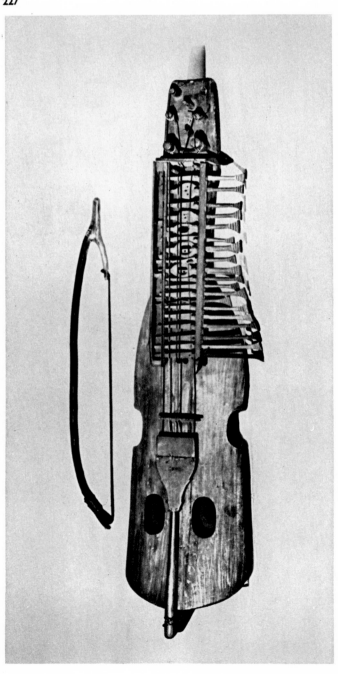

225. Swedish zither *hummel*

226. Swedish peasant with *nyckelharpa*

227. Swedish bowed hurdy-gurdy *nyckelharpa*

228. Prague street musician Josef Häusler with harp

229

229. Moravian children with ratchet and clapper

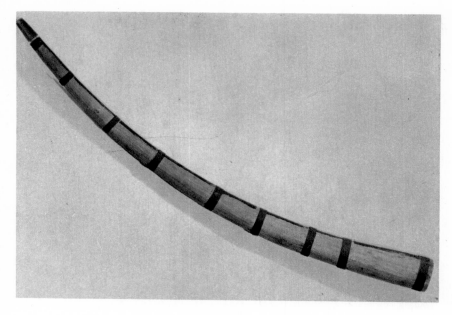

230

230. Polish shepherd's horn *trombita*

231. Polish shepherd's trumpet

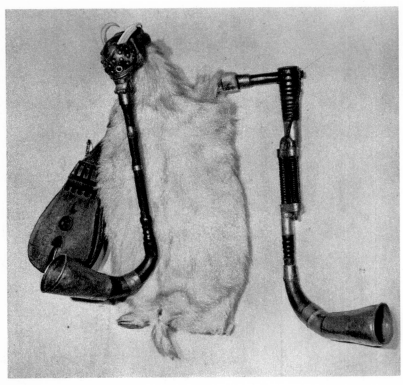

232

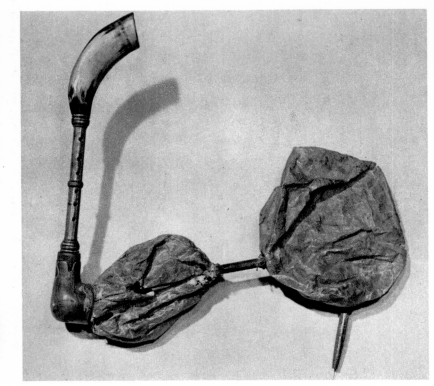

233

234

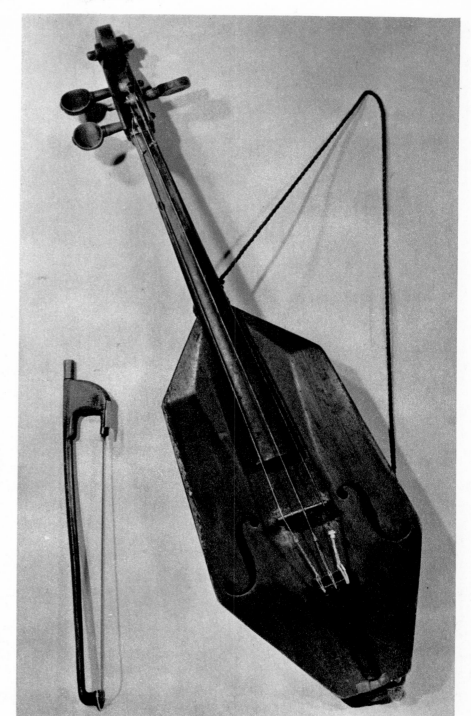

236

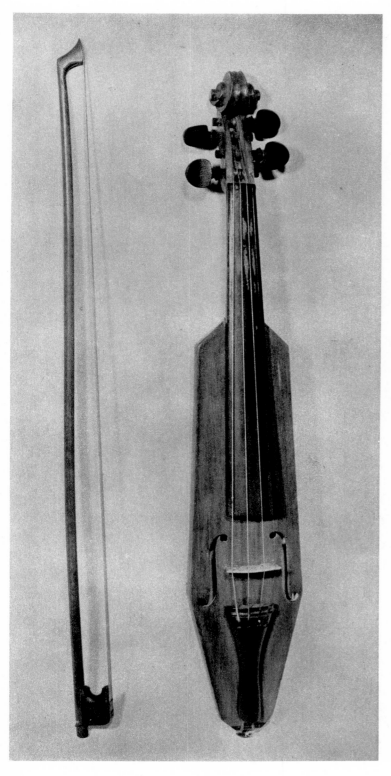

235

232. Polish bagpipe *koza vielkopolska*

233. Polish mouth-blown bagpipe *siesienki*

234. Polish *trabita*

235.—236. Polish folk violin and contrabass

237. Slovak *fujara* and double-flute *dvojachka*

238. Slovak folk instruments

239. Slovak shepherd with flute

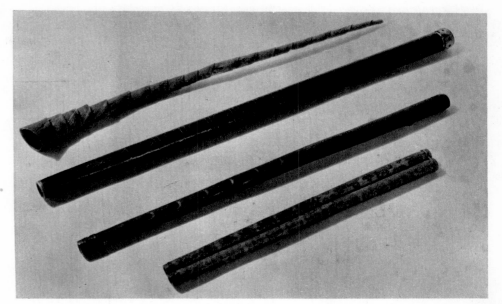

240. Slovak flute *lieskova pishtala*

241.—242. Production of Slovak flutes

243. Etching of ornaments on Slovak folk instruments

242

243

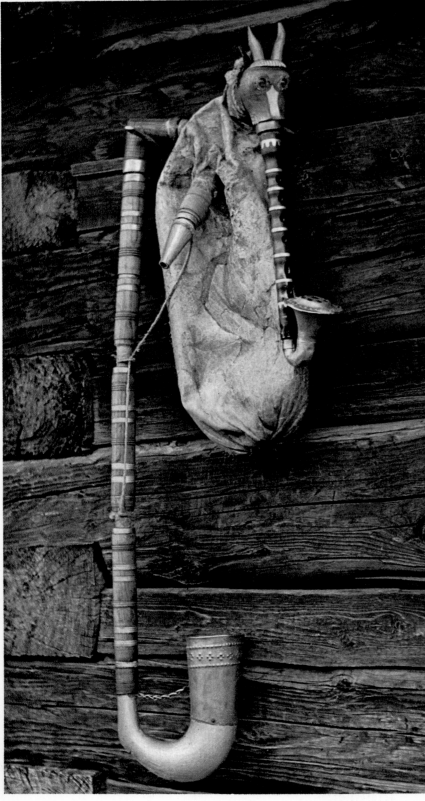

244

245

246

247

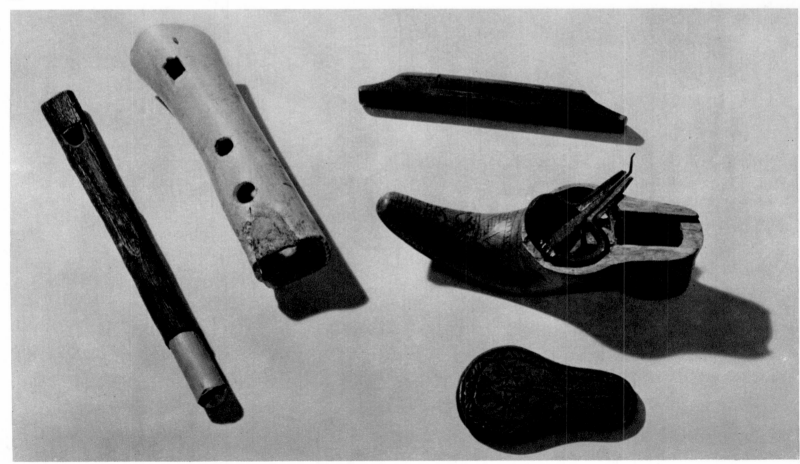

248. Blind hurdy-gurdy player (Bohemia)

249. Hurdy-gurdy from Moravia (Czechoslovakia)

250. Hungarian peasant with zither
251. Hungarian flute *hosszi furulya*

252

253

252. Rumanian shepherd's horn *bucium*

253. Rumanian musician playing the *kobza*

254. Rumanian pan-pipe *nai*

254

255. Bulgarian ensemble of flutes *kaval*

256

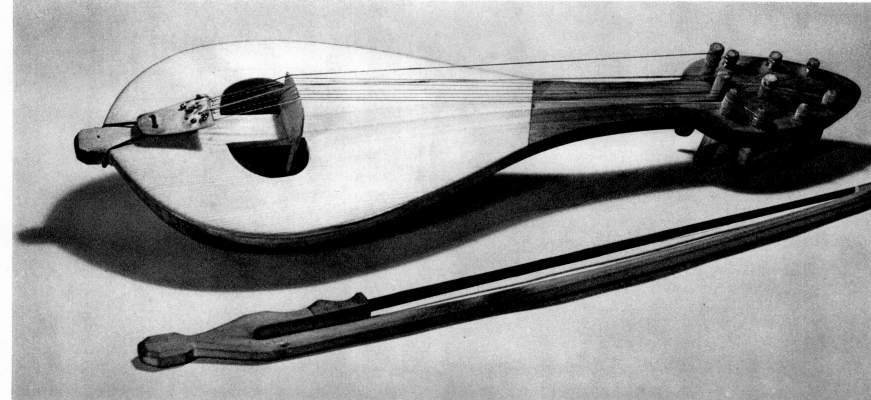

257

258

256. Bulgarian folk musicians with *gadulkas* and *tambura*

257. Bulgarian fiddle *gadulka*

258. Bulgarian bagpipe and *tupan*

259

260

261

259.—260. South Slav double flutes *dvojnitse*

261. Serbian peasant with shepherd's flute

262. Bulgarian ensemble of folk instruments

263. Croatian ensemble of folk instruments

264

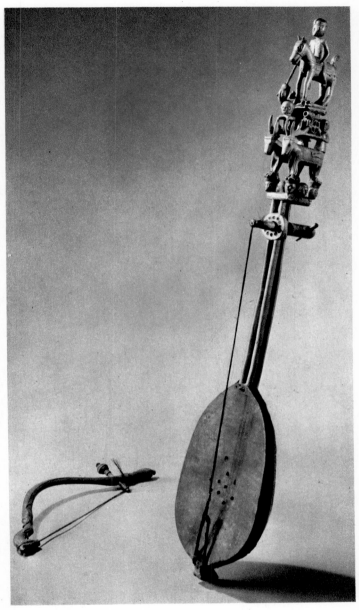

266

264. Yugoslav musician playing shawm *zurla*

265.—266. Yugoslav *gusle* and detail of scroll

265

267. Yugoslav bagpipe player

268

268. Greek lute *uti* and bowed *liraki*

269

270

269. Cretan *lira*

270. Mytilene drum *tarabuka*

271. Greek street musicians

Le Vieilleux.
Der Leyermañ.

273

Le Provencal.
Ein Provencer.

274

272. Greek drummer with *dauli*

273. Musician playing hurdy-gurdy

274. Provençal piper with *galoubet* and *tambourin*

275

275. Moravian bagpipe player

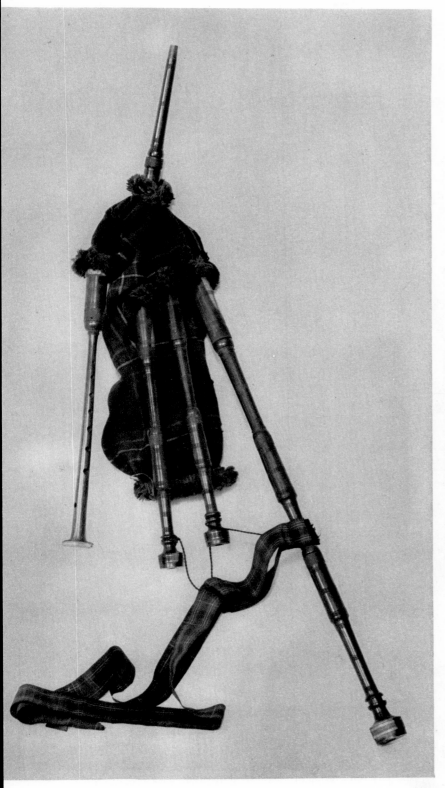

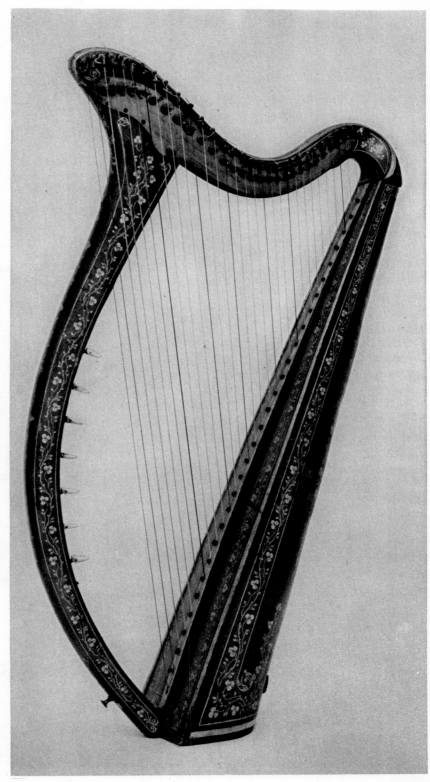

276. Scottish bagpipe

277. Irish harp

278

280

278. Basque whistle *txistu* and small drum *tamboril*

279. Portuguese guitar

280. Basque aerophone *alboka*

281. Basque *txalaparta*

282. Basque accordion *trikitixa* and small drum *yotzale*

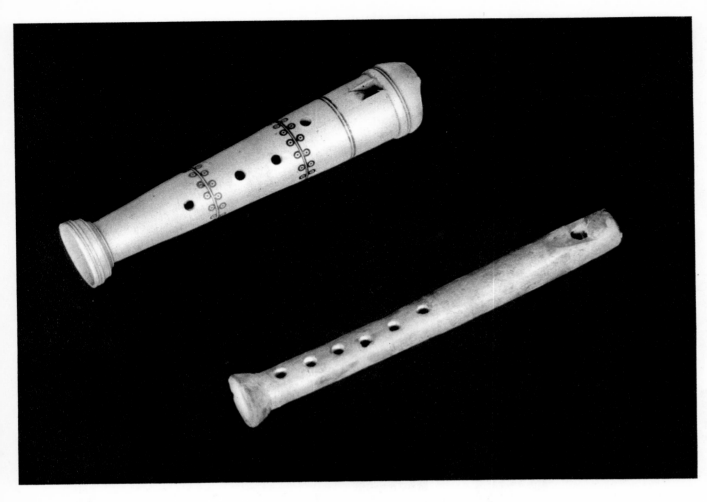

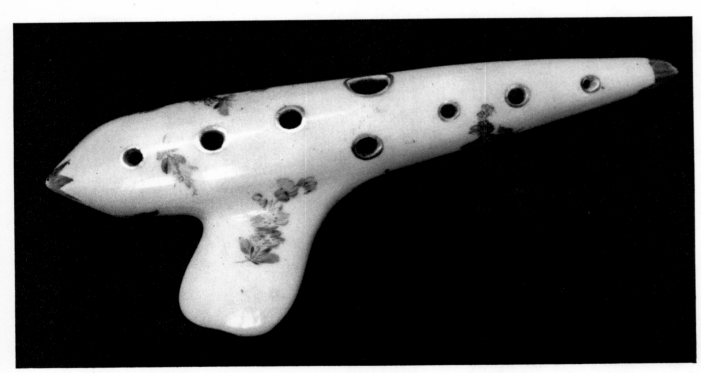

283. French end-blown flutes

284. Ocarina

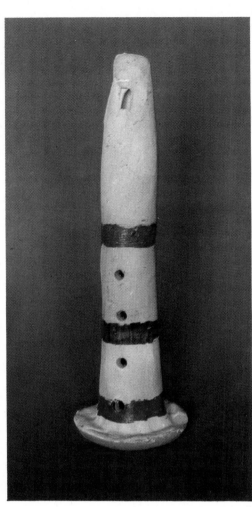

285

286

285. Portuguese end-blown flute

286. Ceramic whistles from Majorca

287. Basque musician playing *alboka*

LIST OF ILLUSTRATIONS

111. *Marimba* from Guatemala
112. Whistling pot *silbador* from Colombia in the shape of an animal playing a pan-pipe. Horniman Museum, London
113. South American bone flute decorated with insect wings (*Chrysophora chysochloa*). Náprstek Museum, Prague
114. South American with pan-pipe
115. Metal covered horn from Bolivia. Náprstek Museum, Prague
116. 'Músicos de madera' (wooden musicians) from the region of Altiplana (Bolivia) with drums and pan-pipes *sicus*
117. Bolivian Indians with flutes *ujusinis*
118. Bolivian Indians with horns *pututu*
119. South American Indian with guitar *charango* made from the scaly shell of an armadillo
120. Drums of the North American Indians. Náprstek Museum, Prague
121. C. Norris of Atlanta playing six different instruments simultaneously

AFRICA

122. Rattles of the Mangbetu tribe (Northern Congo). Náprstek Museum, Prague
123. Rattles from Ubangi Shari (Congo). Náprstek Museum, Prague
124. Metal clapper and calabash rattle from Nigeria
125. Double hand bell made of iron (Congo). Náprstek Museum, Prague
126. Calabash rattle from Nigeria. Horniman Museum, London
127. *Sansas* of the Duala tribe (Cameroon). Náprstek Museum, Prague
128. *Sansas* from the Cameroon and South Africa. Horniman Museum, London
129. Friction drum of the Luvale (Northern Rhodesia). Horniman Museum, London
130. Slit drum from the Congo. Náprstek Museum, Prague
131. Single-membrane drum of the Burundu (West Africa). Horniman Museum, London
132. Kettle drum on the head of a religious statuette with the motif of a snake (ba Kango people in the Central Congo). Horniman Museum, London
133. Drummer of the Babira tribe (Congo)
134. One-headed drum with a motif of lizards from Nigeria. Horniman Museum, London
135. Kettle-drum from Somaliland. Náprstek Museum, Prague
136. 'Speaking drum' *kalangu* of Nigeria. Horniman Museum, London
137.—138. One-headed drums from the Ivory Coast (Baule tribe). Náprstek Museum, Prague
139.—140. Drummers from Dahomey
141.—142. Drummers from Nigeria
143. Flute of the Bagirmi tribe (Nigeria). Horniman Museum, London
144. Bone flute of the Macusi tribe (British Guiana). Horniman Museum, London
145. Ethiopian shepherd from Lake Tana with end-blown flute
146. *Crowd surrounding the drummer*. Coloured wood sculpture from West Africa (Bacongo). Náprstek Museum, Prague
147. Big drums *nagarit* and rattles *tsnasin* at the feast of the Emperor Haile Selassie I. Folk painting. Náprstek Museum, Prague
148. Wooden horn from West Africa. Horniman Museum, London
149. Tube zithers *valiha* from Madagascar. Horniman Museum, London
150. Angular harp from Gaboon
151. Detail of the scroll of angular harp from Gaboon. Horniman Museum, London
152. Lyre from Uganda. Horniman Museum, London
153. Musician from Gaboon with angular harp
154. Board zither *totombito* of the Bandak tribe (Congo). Private collection, Prague
155. Musician of the Kakamega tribe (Kenya) playing the lyre
156. Large Ethiopian lyre *bagana*. Private collection, London

ARABIC COUNTRIES

157. Drum and harp. Iranian miniature. Teheran State Collection
158. Goblet drum *darboka* of glazed terracotta, from Tunis. Náprstek Museum, Prague
159. Iraqi flautist
160. Syrian musician with shawm *zamr*
161. Performance on the double clarinet *zummarah*
162. Bagpipe *zukra* from Saudi Arabia. Horniman Museum, London
163. Iraqi musician with the lute *'ud*
164. Performance on the zither *kanun*
165. Syrian musician with *rabab*
166. Dulcimer *santir* from Iraq
167. Double drum *naqqara*
168. Drum from central Sudan. Náprstek Museum, Prague
169. Iraqi musician with the tambourine *bendir*
170. Tuareg woman (Algiers) with drum
171. Syrian dance with castanets *sunuj* accompanied by a lute
172. Beggar from Tunis with *rabab*
173. Performance on the goblet drum *darboka* (*deblek*)
174. Goblet drum *darboka* from Iraq
175. Nineteenth century Turkish drum *deblek*. Horniman Museum, London
176. Persian drum *darabukke* (*darabuka*). Náprstek Museum, Prague
177. Turkish musician playing the metal flute *sari maden caval*
178. Double clarinets *zummarah*. Náprstek Museum, Prague
179. Turkish musician with shawm *zurna*
180. Boy from south Turkey with beak flute *dillidüdük*
181. Turkish musician with plucked chordophone *saz* (*baglama*)
182. Turkish musician with spike fiddle *kabak kemanje*
183. Nineteenth century Turkish zither *kanun*. Horniman Museum, London
184. Musician with goblet drum *deblek* of southern Turkey

THE SOVIET UNION

185. Tuvinian woman with bowed *pyzanchi*
186. Tuvinian instrumental ensemble. Left to right: bowed *pyzanchi*, guitars *topshulur*, flute *lemba*, bowed *morin chur*
187. Buryat musicians with violin *khuuchir* and flute *limba*
188. Tuvinian woman singing to the accompaniment of the *pyzanchi*
189. Kazakh folk artist Kamar Kasymov, listening to the bowed *kobyz* he made himself
190. Performance on the Kachinz zither *chatchan* (*chat'han*)
191. Ashug Izim Ashimov with *dutar*, Kazakhstan
192. Azerbaijan folk singers P. Panachov (right) and V. Guliyev with *dutar*
193. Instrument maker's workshop at Dushanbe, the capital of Tadzhikistan: chordophones *dutar* (held by the maker), *dumburak* and various types of *tanbur*
194. Kazakh instrument maker M. Safoyev with his instruments: *dombra* (which he is holding) and *tamburina* (held by the girl)
195. Uzbek singer with string instrument *tar*
196. Daghestan musicians with drums *baraban*
197. South Ossetian woman with *dutar*
198. Piper playing the Mari bagpipe *shuvyr*
199. Bronze trumpet *karnaj* and tambourine *dojra* at Tashkent, the capital of Uzbekistan
200. Turkmenian folk musicians. Left to right: spike fiddle *gidzhak* and plucked *dutars*
201. Uzbek fiddle *kemanje*, pupil and teacher
202. Kirghiz chordophone *kiyak*. Constructed by A. I. Petrosyanec and S. E. Didenko in 1955
203. Kirghiz tambourine *dojra*. Náprstek Museum, Prague
204. Uzbek shawm *surnaj*. Museum of Folk Art, Tashkent
205. Uzbek dulcimer *chang*. Museum of Folk Art, Tashkent
206. Uzbek group of musicians with national instruments from Adishan. Left: tambourine *dojra*, violin *rubab*, dulcimer *chang* and guitar *tar*
207. Usta Koman Zuffarow, maker of the Uzbek *rubab*
208. Kazakh women playing *domra*
209. Mari *gusle* and its maker Shtepanovich Kasutin
210. Ensemble of Russian *gusle* players
211. Ensemble of Russian *harmonika* players
212. Ensemble of Tyrolese wind instruments including alto and tenor brass horns with free reeds. Tarnopol region of the Ukraine
213. Estonian boy with shepherd's trumpet *karjapazun*
214. Transcarpathian *sopilkas*, Ukraine
215. Ukrainian *banduras*, Tarnopol region
216. Byelorussian women with dulcimers

EUROPE

217. Norwegian zither *langeleik*
218. Eivind Groven from Telemark, Norway, playing the violin *hardangerfele*
219. Horn *paimensarvi* from Finland. National Museum, Helsinki
220. Five-string *kantele* (archaic shape) from central Finland. National Museum, Helsinki
221. Finnish woman with *kantele*
222.—224. Norwegian violin *hardangerfele* with case
225. Swedish zither *hummel*. Museum of the History of Music, Stockholm
226. Village musician from Uppland, Sweden with *nyckelharpa*
227. Bowed hurdy-gurdy from Sweden. National Museum, Prague
228. Prague street harp-player Josef Häusler. Oil painting by Severin Pfalz (1796—?). Private collection, Prague
229. Moravian children with ratchet and clapper
230. Polish shepherd's horn *trombita*. Museum of Folk Culture and Art, Warsaw
231. Polish folk instrument maker and musician J. Kawulok with shepherd's trumpet
232. Polish bagpipe *koza vielkopolska*. Museum of Folk Culture and Art, Warsaw
233. Polish bagpipe *siesienki* with double bag. Museum of Folk Culture and Art, Warsaw
234. Polish *trabita*
235.—236. Polish folk violin and contrabass. Museum of Folk Culture and Art, Warsaw
237. Slovak *fujara* and double-flute *dvojachka*
238. Slovak folk instruments: *dvojachka*, *flauta*, *koncovka* and reed pipe (bottom to top)
239. Slovak shepherd with *flauta* from Detva
240. Slovak block flute *lieskova pishtala*. Pipe wound with cherry bark
241. Lathe-turned Slovak flute
242. Marking of points where fingerholes must be bored on Slovak flute
243. Etching of ornaments on the tubes of Slovak folk instruments
244. Slovak bagpipes *gajdy*
245. Slovak bells of sheet metal
246. Zither from south Slovakia
247. Slovak folk instruments: signal whistle *pishtala*, whistle of rag-and-bone men *handrlácká*, Jew's harp *brnkachka* in boot-shaped case. Slovak National Museum Martin, (ethnographic section)
248. Blind man with hurdy-gurdy, Bohemia
249. Seventeenth century hurdy-gurdy, Moravia (Czechoslovakia). Moravian Museum, Brno
250. Hungarian musician playing zither from Cigand
251. Hungarian end-blown flute *hosszi furulya* (long flute) from Danube region
252. Rumanian shepherd's horn *bucium*
253. Rumanian musician playing the lute *kobza*
254. Rumanian virtuoso Fanica Luca playing the pan-pipe *nai*
255. Bulgarian ensemble with 139 players on the flute *kaval*
256. Bulgarian folk musicians with *gadulkas* and *tambura*
257. Bulgarian fiddle *gadulka*
258. Bulgarian bagpipe and drum *tupan*
259.—260. South Slav double flutes *dvojnitse*. Ethnographic Museum, Prague
261. Serbian peasant with shepherd's flute
262. Bulgarian ensemble of folk instruments. Left to right: flute *kaval*, *dudy*, *gadulka*, tambourine and a group of *tamburas* with bass *tambura*

284

263. Croatian ensemble of folk instruments. Left to right: guitar, contrabass and tamburas
264. Yugoslav musician on the shawm *zurla*
265.—266. Yugoslav *gusle* and detail of the scroll. National Museum, Prague
267. Bagpipe player from Banat, Yugoslavia
268. Village musicians from Greece, lute *uti* and bowed *liraki*
269. Cretan *lira*, 1743. Museum of Folk Art, Athens
270. Mytilene drum *tarabuka*, Greece. Museum of Folk Art, Athens
271. Greek street musicians with drum *dauli* and shawm *caramuza*
272. Greek folk musician with drum *dauli*
273.—274. Musician playing hurdy-gurdy and Provençal piper on the *galoubet* and *tambourin*. Eighteenth century colour etchings. National Museum, Prague
275. Moravian bagpipe (Czechoslovakia)
276. Scottish bagpipe, 1800. Horniman Museum, London
277. Irish harp by Edgan, Dublin 1820. Horniman Museum, London
278. Basque whistle *txistu* and small drum *tamboril*
279. Portuguese guitar. Horniman Museum, London
280. Basque aerophone *alboka*. Horniman Museum, London
281. Basque *txalaparta*
282. Basque accordion *trikitixa* and small drum *yotzale*
283. French beaked flutes, one of ivory and one of terracotta. Horniman Museum, London
284. Eighteenth century *ocarina* of Meissen porcelain. Horniman Museum, London
285. Portuguese end-blown flute of terracotta. Horniman Museum, London
286. Ceramic whistles from Majorca. One in the traditional horseman shape, the other in the shape of a motorcyclist. Horniman Museum, London
287. Basque *alboka* player, Mariano Barrenechea

BIBLIOGRAPHY

AARFLOT, O.: *Kinesisk musikk*. Oslo 1948
АЛЕНДЕР, И. З.: *Музыкальные инструменты*. Москва 1958
ALEXANDRU, T.: *Instrumentale muzicale ale poporului romin*. Bucharest 1956
ANDERSEN, J. C.: *Maori Music with its Polynesian Background*. New Plymouth 1934
ARBATSKY, Y.: *Beating the Tupan in the Central Balkans*. Chicago 1953
ARETZ, I.: *Instrumentos musicales de Venezuela*. Cumaná 1967
AYERSTARÁN, L.: *Música en el Uruguay*. Montevideo 1953
BAINES, A.: *Bagpipes*. Oxford 1960
BALOCH, N. A.: *Musical Instruments of the Lower Indus Valley of Sind*. Hyderabad 1966
BANDOPADHYAYA, S.: *The Music of India*. Bombay 1945
BOSE, F.: *Musikalische Völkerkunde*. Freiburg 1956
BRANDEL, R.: *The Music of Central Africa*. Den Haag 1961
BRÖMSE, P.: *Flöten, Schalmeien und Sackpfeifen Südslaviens*. Brno 1937
BUCHNER, A.: *Musical Instruments Through the Ages*. Prague 1956
BUCHNER, A.: *Hornimanovo muzeum a problémy etnoorganologie*. Praha ČNM 1965
CARRINGTON, J. F.: *Talking Drums of Africa*. London 1949
CHAUVET, ST.: *Musique nègre*. Paris 1929
COLLAER, P.: *Ozeanien (Musikgeschichte in Bildern)*. Leipzig 1965
COLLAER, P.: *Amerika (Musikgeschichte in Bildern)*. Leipzig 1967
DANIÉLOU, A.: *La Musique du Cambodge et du Laos*. Pondichéry 1957
DHANIT, Y.: *Thai Musical Instruments*. Bangkok 1957
Die Musik in Geschichte und Gegenwart. Kassel 1949—68
DURIYANGA, P. C.: *Thai Music*. Bangkok 1954
ECKARDT, A.: *Koreanische Musik*. Tokyo 1930
Encyclopédie de la musique. Paris 1958—61
FARMER, H. G.: *Studies in Oriental Musical Instruments*. Glasgow 1939
FARMER, H. G.: *The Music and Musical Instruments of the Arab*. London 1914
FARMER, H. G.: *Turkish Instruments in the 17th Century*. Glasgow 1937
FISCHER, H.: *Schallgeräte in Ozeanien*. Strassbourg 1958
GOSVAMI, O.: *The Story of Indian Music*. Bombay 1957
Grove's Dictionary of Music and Musicians. London 1954
GÜNTHER, R.: *Musik in Rwanda*. Tervueren 1964
D'HARCOURT, M. et R.: *La musique des Aymars sur les Hauts Plateaux Boliviens*. Paris 1959
D'HARCOURT, M. et R.: *La musique des Incas et ses survivances*. Paris 1925
HOLAS, B.: *Arts de la Côte d'Ivoire*. Paris 1966
IZIKOWITZ, K. G.: *Musical and Other Sound Instruments of the South American Indians*. Gothenborg 1935
JENKINS, J.: *Musical Instruments*. London 1958
JONES, A. M.: *Studies in African Music*. London 1959
KAUDERA, W.: *Musical Instruments in Celebes*. Gothenborg 1927
KIRBY, P. R.: *The Musical Instruments of the Native Races of South Africa*. London 1934
KIRBY, P. R.: *The Reed-Flute Ensembles of South Africa*. London 1933
KUNST, J.: *Study on Papuan Music*. Weltevreden 1931
KUNST, J.: *Hindoe-Javaansche Muziek-Instrumenten speciaal die van oost-Java*. Weltevreden 1927
KUNST, J.: *Music in Java*. Den Haag 1949
KWABENA NKEITA, J. H.: *African Music in Ghana*. Accra 1961
KYAGAMBIDWA, J.: *African Music from the Source of the Nile*. London 1956
LANGE DE, M. M.: *Catalogue of the Musical Instruments in the Collection of Prof. Percival R. Kirby*. Johannesburg 1967
LAURENTY, J. S.: *Les chordofones du Congo Belge et du Ruanda-Urundi*. Tervueren 1960
LAURENTY, J. S.: *Les sanza du Congo*. Tervueren 1962
LENG, L.: *Slovenské ľudové hudobné nástroje*. Bratislava 1967
LING, J.: *Nyckelharpan*. Stockholm 1967
MALM, W. P.: *Japanese Music and Musical Instruments*. Rutland 1960
MARCUSE, S.: *Musical Instruments. A comprehensive Dictionary*. New York 1964
MARTÍ, S.: *Instrumentos Musicales Precortesianos*. Mexico City 1955
MC PHEE, C.: *Music in Bali*. New Haven-London 1966
MUKERJI, D. P.: *Indian Music*. Bombay 1945
New Oxford History of Music. London 1957—66
ORTIZ, F.: *Los instrumentos de la música Afrocubana*. Habana 1952-55
PIGGOTT, F.: *The Music and Musical Instruments of Japan*. London 1909
PISCHNER, H.: *Musik in China*. Berlin 1955
REINHARD, K.: *Chinesische Musik*. Kassel 1956
ROSENTHAL, E.: *The Story of Indian Music and its Instruments*. London 1928
SACHS, C.: *Geist und Werden der Musikinstrumente*. Berlin 1929
SACHS, C.: *Les instruments de musique de Madagascar*. Paris 1938
SACHS, C.: *The History of Musical Instruments*. New York 1940
SACHS, C.: *Die Musikinstrumente Birmas und Assams*. München 1917
SACHS, C.: *Die Musikinstrumente Indiens und Indonesiens*. Berlin 1915
SACHS, C.: *Reallexikon der Musikinstrumente*. Berlin 1913
SACHS, C.: *Handbuch der Musikinstrumentenkunde*. Berlin 1920
SÁROSI, B.: *A magyar nép hangszerei*. Budapest 1965
SHARPE, A. P. A.: *Complete Guide to the Instruments of the Banjo Family*. New York—London 1966
SÖDERBERG, B.: *Les instruments de musique du Bas-Congo et dans les régions avoisinantes*. Stockholm 1956
STEVENSON, R.: *The Music of Peru*. Washington 1959
SUNAGA, K.: *Japanese Music*. Tokyo 1936
TRACEY, H.: *Chopi Musicians, their Music and Instruments*. London 1948
TRAN VAN KHÉ: *La musique vietnamienne traditionnelle*. Paris 1962
TSAI-PING LIANG: *Chinese Music*. Taipei 1955
U KHIN ZAW: *Burmese Music. The Open Mind*. Burma 1961
VEGA, C.: *Los Instrumentos musicales aborígenes y criollos de la Argentina*. Buenos Aires 1943

ВЕРТКОВ, К., ВЛАГОДАТОВ, Г., ЯЗОВИЦКАЯ, Е.: *Атлас музыкальных инструментов народов СССР,* Москва 1963
WALIN, S.: *Die schwedische Hummel.* Stockholm 1952
WEINSTOCK, H.: *Mexican Music.* New York 1940
WIESCHOFF, H.: *Die Afrikanischen Trommeln und ihre Außerafrikanischen Beziehungen.* Stuttgart 1933
WILLIAMS, F. E.: *Bull-roarers in the Papuan Gulf.* Port Moresby 1936
WINTERNITZ, E.: *Musical Instruments of the Western World.* London 1966
WIRZ, P.: *A Description of Musical Instruments from Central North-Eastern New Guinea.* Amsterdam 1952
WÜNSCH, W.: *Die Geigentechnik der südslawischen Guslaren.* Brno 1934

ACKNOWLEDGMENTS

The following pictures are reproduced by kind permission of:
Bremme de Santos, I., Guatemala City: 111
Buchner, A., Prague: 2—10, 12, 16—17, 19—20, 24, 28—29, 40, 42—43, 45, 47—51, 53—56, 59, 63—64, 87, 92—96, 108—109, 112—113, 115, 120, 122—123, 125—132, 134—138, 143—144, 146—152, 154, 156—159, 162, 168, 175—176, 178, 183, 203, 222—224, 227—229, 248, 259—260, 273—277, 279—280, 283—286 (with kind permission of the Horniman Museum, London)
Centre of Artistic Folk Creation, Bratislava: 240—245
Československá tisková kancelář, Prague: 105, 226, 239
Credit-Herbert Photos: 53
Cuban Ministry of Culture, Havana: 107
Dabac, T., Zagreb: 261, 263—266, 267
Daniélou, A., Archives of the International Institute for Comparative Music Studies and Documentation, Berlin: 70—73, 75, 77, 79—80, 82—83, 85, 88
Ethnographical Museum, Bucharest: 252—254
Hanzelka, J. — Zikmund, M., Gottwaldov-Zlín: 106, 110, 114, 119
Hilmerová, O., Prague: 238, 246—247, 249
Historical Music Museum, Stockholm: 225
Hombek, H., Wisla: 231, 234
Honty, T., Prague: 265—266
Institute of Bulgarian Ethnography, Sofia: 255—258, 262
Iraq Ministry of Culture, Baghdad: 159, 161, 163—164, 166—167, 169, 173—174
Jairasbhoy, N. A., London: 44, 52, 62, 65—69
Jenkins, J., London: 124
Jisl, L., Prague: 38—39, 41
Jonsborg, K., Oslo: 217—218
Korean Institute of Culture, Phonyang: 30
Meletzne, B., Athens: 268—272
Musée de l'Homme, Paris; photographers *Benezech, Cl. J., Fouquet, Cl. G., Zurov, Cl.:* 171—172, 213
Museum of Folk Art, Warsaw: 230, 232—236
Náprstek Museum, Prague; photographer *Machulka, B.:* 133
National Museum, Helsinki; photographer *Kanerva, V. T.:* 219—221
New China Press Agency, Peking: 11, 13—15, 18
Paul, A., Prague: 237
Petrosjanc, A. I., Tashkent: 202, 204—205
Press Information Bureau, Government of India, New Delhi: 46, 57, 60—61
Rapho, Paris: 139—140, 145, 153
Reinhard, K., Berlin: 177, 179—182, 184
Royal Tropics Institute, Amsterdam: 86
Sáez, Bilbao: 278, 281—282, 287
Sárosi, B., Budapest: 251
Society for International Cultural Contacts, Tokyo: 31—37
Šolc, V., Prague: 116—118
State Institute for Culture, Phnom Penh, Cambodia: 74, 76, 78, 81, 84
Syrian Ministry of Culture, Damascus: 160, 165
Tass, Moscow; photographers *Boyko, G., Kunov, V., Lagranzh, V., Mustafina, K., Trepetova, B., Pozdenko, V., Rachil, J., Shendler, B., Voytenko, V.:* 185—198, 200—201, 208—212, 214—220
Uztag, Tashkent; photographer *Masura, B.:* 199, 206—207
Vaniš-Sís, Prague: 21, 25—27, 89—91, 93
Western Nigeria Service, London: 141—142
Younitzky, P., Paris: 121

DRAWINGS IN THE TEXT

Aleš, M., Prague
Belyayev, V., Moscow
Bobri, V., New York
Buchner, A., Prague
Capdeville, J., Mexico
Kass, J., Budapest
Kodzhoyan, A., Jerevan
King, H., USA
Konečná, M., Prague
Maira, G., Wellington
Petrov, M., Moscow
Valls, J., Havana

INDEX